Morning Meditations

A Daily Devotional Guide For Musicians

by
Alexander D. Marini
(harp maker)

MORNING MEDITATIONS
A DAILY DEVOTIONAL GUIDE FOR MUSICIANS

Library of Congress Number: 2006937903

International Standard Book Number: 1-60126-008-3

Printed 2006 at
Masthof Press
219 Mill Road
Morgantown, PA 19543-9516

TABLE OF CONTENTS

Part 5: Spiritual Gifts

Part 6: Godly Music

Part 7: The Worship Atmosphere

ABOUT THE AUTHOR

I can't play the harp, or any other instrument, and I'm not a great singer. I have no formal training in music, in fact, I can't even read notes. So who am I to write a devotional guide for musicians? Well, I've been making harps since 1995. My two oldest daughters, Dena and Joanna, are extremely gifted harpists and have made seven recordings so far. We've given hundreds of harp programs at which I speak on various topics related to harps and music, with much emphasis on the spiritual aspects of harp usage and music. And I have shared devotionals for a couple years at our monthly harp workshop which we offer free to anyone interested in using the harp for ministry. Finally, and most important, I have been a serious student of the Bible since 1974, and our involvement with harps has sparked a keen interest in all the Bible has to say about them, and music in general. That's my harp and music-related background. Otherwise, I'm a part-time high school Health and Wood Shop teacher. I have a faithful wife, Sue, and six children whom we homeschool. As a family, we attend a non-denominational church called Ephrata Christian Fellowship.

PREFACE

I suppose I always knew that within every human lies a spiritual dimension. Beyond physical, beyond intellectual, a part of our being seeks to know--to be one with the "Source" of life. Once that "Source" is found, worship inevitably results. This compulsion to worship finds its expression in various forms, but I know no higher form than music, and particularly, the blending of harp and voice. Other instruments have a wonderful place in worship as well, but, as you might have already gathered, I have particular affinity for harps, which will be obvious throughout this book. In fact, this book started out focusing solely on the harp, but so much of it seemed applicable to all musicians that I decided to broaden its scope to include other instruments, and singing as well. In different parts of this book the harp will be singled out, but only because the Bible singles it out some times. Admittedly, I am biased toward harps, not only because I make them, and happen to think harps are the sweetest sounding instruments ever developed, but also because they have a very special place in the Bible.

Further, everyone seems to know that there is something special about the harp, something spiritual, something sacred. I count it my sacred privilege to share with you the truths I have discovered in my search for spiritual understanding as it relates to the harp, other instruments, and music in general. I realize, of course, that my spiritual orientation is just one of countless religious views in this new millennium of history. So permit me to share the vantage point from which spring all of my devotionals.

MY SPIRITUAL ORIENTATION

Growing up in a church-going family, I must have been totally oblivious to most spiritual truths that came my way. I basically lived as if God did not exist. By age 20, as a soldier in the army, I denied God's existence. At the same time I realized that I had spent much of my life trying to please my peers. I saw that many of the things I felt pressured into doing were worthless and destructive. So I decided to run my own life and do whatever was right and good in my own eyes, regardless of what others thought. All was well, except for one nagging issue—God. For all the humanistic and atheistic philosophy I tried to develop, the time came when I could no longer deny God's existence. Life must have a "Source," and creation must have a Creator, for nothing gives rise to itself. I knew God was out there, somewhere, but how to find Him amidst such a diverse and confusing array of religions? How could I know which, if any, were true? So I prayed. What else could I do? Asking to be shown the truth, I began reading holy writings: Confucius, Hindu literature, and even the Bible. I told God I was willing and ready to do whatever it took to learn the truth, even if it meant traveling to India to study under a guru.

Then came the messenger, one of God's ambassadors, "born-agains" they're called. He was a rather obnoxious fellow, yet, he seemed to have some truth. He introduced me to a multitude of others like him, who also seemed to have truth. Over the following weeks and months the bits and pieces of truth began to fall together, and the foundational truths of life, death, and eternity became clear. I became frightfully aware of God's obvious presence, looking down at every thought, word and deed of my whole life. I felt like a thief whose crime was captured on video by a hidden camera. Woe unto me! I had spent my life denying His existence and His absolute and awesome power over my fate. Woe unto me! From day one I had defied His rightful authority--indeed, His divine prerogative to tell me what I may and may not do. I stood before Him, speechless, guilty, condemned, without excuse, without justification, and with no ability to make up for a sinful life. I was cornered--what else could I do, but cry for mercy?

But I did not deserve forgiveness. Divine Justice must be satisfied, for Sovereign Law demands payment for sin, as the Bible says: "the wages of sin is death" (Rom 6:23). "Death"--eternal separation from God, and being cast into the fiery hell. "Death"--the only just, fitting, and effective punishment for offending and rebelling against the Most High. What else can God do with sinners who refuse to repent? Shall He infest heaven and endure eternity with a host of defiant, rebellious people inhabiting His dwelling place? Heaven would be no different than this present world of sin and corruption. Shall He cohabit forever with those who will not allow Him to be God, who defy His right to rule? He wouldn't be God if He did. He truly has no choice but to cast them out. And such was my fate, were it not for that blessed messenger, obnoxious as he was. He and his comrades delivered to me a wonderful message from God:

> **"But God commendeth his love toward us, in that,**
> **while we were yet sinners, Christ died for us"**
> **(Rom 5:8).**

What an awesome statement! God still loved me. Though I've denied and defied Him, He still loved me, enough to allow His own Son to take my punishment, to die in my place:

> **"All we like sheep have gone astray; we have turned**
> **every one to his own way; and the Lord hath laid on**
> **him the iniquity of us all" (Isa 53:6).**

From my youth I had been taught that Jesus died for our sins, but His death had never meant anything to me. I could not appreciate His death until now, now that I finally saw the sentence of death that I deserved. There was nothing to do but confess my sins and plead for mercy. And since Jesus was willing to be executed in my place, I gladly repented of my sins and set my heart to please Him. Therefore, I study the Bible to discover God's views of every issue of life, that I may embrace His views, and please Him. And this devotional guide is my attempt to pass God's views on to you, that you might do the same.

How to Use This Guide

Of course, you are free to use this guide any way you like, but here are a few suggestions. This guide is intended to be a "daily" devotional guide. That is, it is divided into relatively small, independent units, enough food-for-thought for one day. I'd suggest that you read one day's material and then take some time to pray and meditate on it. Sometimes when we read a book straight through we miss a lot, and there is little chance to digest what we have read. You might also consider looking up the Bible references cited to study them within their context. Perhaps you will wish to play and sing a song or two that follows the theme of the day's material as part of your worship time.

A Word About *"Devotions"*

We have come to call it "personal devotions," this practice of "devoting" a daily block of time to privately developing our relationship with God. There are many who have no "devotional" life what-so-ever, but all their time and energy is "devoted" to the affairs of this life. Others have chosen to engage in "spiritual" devotions, and practices include anything from a brief reading and/or whispering a 30 second prayer at the start of the day, to extensive sessions of reading, studying, prayer, meditation, singing, instrument playing, and the like. I have no desire to dictate any specific period of time or set of activities for anyone. But somehow we each have to find what is appropriate, effective, and practical for us, because we all need to develop and maintain our relationship with God.

Motivation for Devotions: Too often, I'm afraid, we see devotions as a "discipline," a spiritual duty, or a religious obligation. With such a view we tend to feel guilty if we should miss our devotional time, so we try to force ourselves to be faithful with it. This kind of motivation is alarmingly wide-spread, and I would be most disappointed to discover that my devotional guide should ever be used as a tool to carry on this sort of obligatory devotional life. Perhaps I can best illustrate my discontent with this approach by sharing a little story:

THE PARABLE OF
THE GROOM AND BRIDE-TO-BE

There once was a young man betrothed to a young lady. He so looked forward to their wedding day and spending the rest of his life in the presence of this fine young lady. From the beginning they were enraptured with one another, and jumped at every opportunity to be together. Everything else in life became quite secondary, and sharing one another's company was all that mattered. For those times when they were separated they busied themselves writing love letters, cherishing each one in a safe place.

Now as time progressed and the wedding day approached the young lady began to see the need to focus her attention on certain necessary matters of life: her work, home, friends, so on and so forth. Her visits with her sweetheart became shorter, fewer, and farther between. He began to feel disappointed, then slighted, and understandably so. And it wasn't long before the visits stopped altogether, albeit, the young lady did continue to keep in touch by letter, constantly reassuring her groom-to-be of her profound love for him. Eventually she no longer answered his letters, but simply read the letters he wrote to her.

As you can imagine, in the course of time the young man could stand it no more. Therefore he made known, in no uncertain terms, his displeasure with being neglected so, and his skepticism of her love for him. The young lady, feeling quite guilty, vowed from the bottom of her heart to "discipline" herself to spend more time with him from that day forth. And so she did, for a short time. But alas, she was soon back to devoting her time and attention to anything and everything but her groom-to-be. She even requested that he write shorter letters as they were taking too much time to read.

As one might expect, the young man complained once more with greater intensity, inquiring as to how she expected to maintain a relationship this way. Overwhelmed with guilt and shame, the young lady gritted her teeth, rolled up her sleeves, and stamped her foot, declaring, "That's it! I'm going to force myself to visit with you every day, no matter what!"

Question: How then do you suppose this sat with the young man? Would he be pleased that his bride-to-be intended to "discipline" herself to spend time with him?

Would he be satisfied that she planned to "force" herself to visit him, "no matter what?" Is this an appropriate relationship for a groom and bride-to-be?

The Meaning of the Parable: Does not the Bible teach that we, the church, are indeed the "bride" of Christ, and He the Groom? We are betrothed, and we look forward to that Great Wedding Feast. How then do you suppose it sits with Him when our visits are a matter of "discipline," indeed "forcing" ourselves. Those words carry weighty connotations that suggest displeasure--that we'd much prefer to be doing something else. But out of guilt we feel a need to fulfill this "duty," as if it were a distasteful, oppressive "obligation." How much better to approach devotions as a delight, rather than a duty; a privilege, rather than an obligation; just as an enraptured groom and bride-to-be would view their time together. And rather than feeling "guilt" when circumstances prevent us from having our devotions, how much better to feel disappointment, just as a groom and bride-to-be would.

The Place of Devotional Books: Some resort to using a devotional book such as this one as a time and labor-saving device. It's quicker and easier than reading the Bible, sort of like the bride-to-be requesting that her groom-to-be write shorter letters. And a brief, devotional book reading makes us feel like we've met our spiritual obligations for the day. Yes, reading is important, but reading without prayer and meditation is a lot like the bride-to-be trying to carry on their relationship by reading her fiance's letters without ever responding or visiting. Therefore may I exhort you, above all, do not neglect prayer and meditation, for that is your personal and intimate connection with God. This guide cannot replace that communion, it serves only as a "guide," a collection of points to ponder. God is up there 24 hours a day, longing for your fellowship. The door is open to you any time you want. What an awesome privilege we have! Think of it. We have an open invitation from the God of the universe to make requests of Him through prayer, to discuss all the issues of life with Him through meditation, and to basque in His presence. May I encourage you to set aside a block of time to meet with Him, 20, 40, 60 minutes, whatever is practical for you. Not because you have to, but because you want to enjoy His presence. And use this devotional guide, not as a replacement for prayer and meditation, but simply as an aid to focus your thoughts.

A Word About Prayer and Meditation

We should make a distinction here between Biblical prayer and meditation, and other forms of prayer and meditation that have become popular today. The prayer and meditation that I recommend, that the Bible speaks of, is nothing mysterious, nothing transcendental. The word "prayer" as used in the Bible simply means "to ask," to "make request." Though God already knows what we need and want before we ask, still, He has filled the Bible with exhortations to pray, along with promises to answer. Prayer should be an integral part of everyone's devotional life. And meditation, likewise, should not be neglected. The word "meditation" as used in the Bible simply means "deep thinking." It does not involve some altered state of consciousness, but focused conscious thought, where you think things through and draw reasonable conclusions based on the truths that God has revealed in the Bible. Think of meditation as a conversation with God, a period of "reasoning" with Him. As He called His people, Israel, saying: "Come now, and let us reason together, saith the Lord…." (Isa 1:18), so He calls us to reason with Him about every issue of life.

Benefits of Meditation: It is during periods of prayer and meditation that we are best able to make important decisions.

These are the times when we consider our ways, face truth, come to grips with reality, examine ourselves in light of His commands to us, confess sins, repent, and gain understanding of life. The Bible lists quite a number of specific benefits, here are a few:

- Prosperity and Good Success:

  This book of the law shall not depart out of thy mouth but thou shalt meditate therein day and night, that thou mayest observe to do according to all that is written therein: for then thou shalt make thy way prosperous, and then thou shalt have good success (Josh 1:8).

- Avoid Sin:

  Thy word have I hid in mine heart, that I might not sin against thee (Ps 119:11).

I thought on my ways, and turned my feet unto thy testimonies (Ps 119:59).

- Learn to Love God's Commands, Gain Wisdom and Understanding:

    O how love I thy law! It is my meditation all the day. Thou through thy commandments hast made me wiser than mine enemies: for they are ever with me. I have more understanding than all my teachers: for thy testimonies are my meditation. I understand more than the ancients, because I keep thy precepts. I have refrained my feet from every evil way, that I might keep thy word. I have not departed from thy judgments: for thou hast taught me. How sweet are thy words unto my taste! Yea, sweeter than honey to my mouth! Through thy precepts I get understanding: therefore I hate every false way (Ps 119:97-104).

    I will meditate in thy precepts, and have respect unto thy ways. I will delight myself in thy statutes; I will not forget thy word" (Ps 119:15).

    And I will delight myself in thy commandments, which I have loved. My hand also will lift up unto thy commandments, which I have loved; and I will meditate in thy statutes" (Ps 119:47-48).

We could go on, but hopefully you get the picture. From the beginning, God's desire for mankind has been to enjoy a relationship together. Through sin we broke that relationship. Through Christ's blood, our faith and repentance, that relationship was restored. We have only to maintain that relationship during this life, and prayer and meditation is our primary means. May God grant you wisdom, understanding, holiness, prosperity, and good success.

PART 1

God's Love for Music

"THE LORD IS HIGH ABOVE ALL NATIONS,
AND HIS GLORY ABOVE THE HEAVENS"
(PS 113:4).

1

MUSIC AND HARPS IN HEAVEN

Picture this. We're standing before the throne, the very throne of God! The entire atmosphere of heaven rings with **"the voice of harpers harping with their harps" (Rev 14:2):** a sweet, clear fullness, the likes of which you have never experienced. Before the throne lies a lustrous, glowing **"sea of glass mingled with fire" (Rev 15:2).** On that sea of glass stands a myriad of tribulation overcomers, and every one of them holds, of all things, a harp, the most exquisite, glistening, perfectly designed instruments you have ever seen. Your gaze shifts to the great throne itself. You see it there, **"and one sat on the throne. And he that sat was to look upon like a jasper and a sardine stone: and there was a rainbow round about the throne, in sight like unto an emerald . . . and out of the throne proceeded lightnings and thunderings and voices" (Rev 4:2-5).** And lo, this great throne, God's very throne, is surrounded with no less than 28 harps, held by the four beasts (angelic living ones), and the four and twenty elders. All 28 of them **"fell down before the Lamb, having every one of them harps, and golden vials full of odours, which are the prayers of saints. And they sung a new song, saying, Thou art worthy to take the book, and to open the seals thereof: for thou wast slain, and has redeemed us to God by thy blood out of every kindred, and tongue, and people and nation; And hast made us unto our God kings and priests: and we shall reign on the earth. And I beheld, and heard the voice of many angels round about the throne and the beasts and the elders: and the number of them was ten thousand times ten thousand, and thousands of thousands; Saying with a loud voice, Worthy is the Lamb that was slain to receive power, and riches, and wisdom, and strength, and honour, and glory, and blessing. And every creature which is in heaven, and on the earth, and under the earth, and such as are in the sea, and all that are in them, heard I saying, Blessing, and honour, and glory, and power, be unto him that sitteth upon the throne, and unto the Lamb for ever and ever. And the four beasts said, Amen. And the four and twenty elders fell down and worshipped him that liveth for ever and ever" (Rev 5:8-14).**

That's how the apostle John described it in the Book of Revelation when he was granted the incredible privilege of being taken up into heaven. He saw and heard what goes on up there, and probably recorded only a small portion of the sights and sounds he experienced.

This passage of Scripture is packed with loads of deep and weighty theology, but as a harp maker I can't help but notice that, in the midst of this wondrous record, John did not overlook the presence of music in heaven, and particularly, the harp. Indeed, he is careful to mention the harps of heaven no less than three times. I wondered then, "Why is it that harps and harp music proliferate so in God's abode?" And it occurred to me—"Well, obviously, God must like music, and especially harp music." In fact, I'm convinced that the harp is God's favorite instrument, because there are no other instruments mentioned for worship in heaven. The trumpet is mentioned in heaven, but that was used only for announcements. But when it comes to worship in heaven, the harp takes it, hands down. Other instruments have their place in earthly worship, be assured, and blessed is the musician who seeks to honor God with his music. But more blessed are you, O harp player, for you play God's favorite instrument. Join King David, the man after God's own heart, in blessing and ministering to the Lord:

> **"Then will I go unto the altar of God, unto God my exceeding joy: yea, upon the harp will I praise thee, O God my God" (Ps 43:4).**

2

THE TWO SIDES OF MUSIC

Here I was, in my forties, a Christian for over two decades, and it had never occurred to me that God enjoys music. Maybe that's old hat to you, but this was fresh revelation for me. It wasn't until I got involved with harps that I began to notice God's delight in harps, and music in general. I had always thought of music as a horizontal thing, you know, something we do for our own pleasure, our own edification, and there is that side to music:

> **Let the word of Christ dwell in you richly in all wisdom;**
> **teaching and admonishing one another in psalms and hymns**
> **and spiritual songs, singing with grace in your hearts to the**
> **Lord (Col 3:16).**

So we are instructed here to **"teach and admonish one another"** with music. That's horizontal. But in this same verse we also have the vertical aspect of music where we are told to sing **"to the Lord."** Our music is to be directed up to Him, for His listening pleasure. We find similar instruction elsewhere in the New Testament:

> **Speaking to yourselves in psalms and hymns and spiritual**
> **songs, singing and making melody in your heart to the**
> **Lord (Eph 5:19).**

Again, we see both sides of music here. **"Speaking to yourselves,"** the horizontal side, and **"to the Lord,"** the vertical side. The Old Testament brings out this thought as well:

> **O come, let us sing unto the Lord: let us make a joyful noise**
> **to the rock of our salvation. Let us come before his presence**
> **with thanksgiving, and make a joyful noise unto him with**
> **psalms (Ps 95:1-2).**

> **Sing unto God, sing praises to his name: extol him that**
> **rideth upon the heavens by his name JAH, and rejoice**
> **before him (Ps 68:4).**

Notice how the music is all directed up to God, for His listening pleasure, as a blessing for Him. I'm afraid I'd have to confess that, sometimes, too many times, I'm not conscious of God's listening ear when I make music. Too much focus on other things, other people, perhaps even the quality of my music, tends to prevent God's listening presence from even entering my mind. And I suspect I'm not the only one who struggles to remain aware that I'm supposed to be doing music for God's pleasure. Although, we do have reason to believe that in days-gone-by God's people perhaps were more conscious of this. The Roman historian, Pliny, wrote of the Christians of the second century:

"they met at day break to sing an hymn to one, Christ, as God."

Isn't that beautiful? Can't you just picture these early Christians gathering first thing in the morning, perhaps in the woods somewhere? And the purpose of their gathering? Simply to sing a hymn to the Saviour, for His listening pleasure, just to bless Him with a song. It seems to me they must have been keenly aware that He was listening, He was their audience, and this was one way they could be a blessing to Him. O for this kind of God-consciousness, be it during a church service, family worship time, or personal devotional time:

Sing unto God, sing praises to his name: extol him that rideth upon the heavens by his name JAH, and rejoice before him (Ps 68:4).

3

Music in Creation

Have you ever noticed how many things in Creation that God calls to make music? He must really enjoy it. He even calls inanimate things to sing:

> **Sing, O ye heavens; for the Lord hath done it: shout, ye**
> **lower parts of the earth: break forth into singing, ye**
> **mountains, O forest, and every tree therein (Isa 44:23).**

The sky, the earth, mountains, the forest and every tree in it, all are commanded to sing. Joining their chorus we find the pastures and valleys:

> **The pastures are clothed with flocks; the valleys also are**
> **covered over with corn; they shout for joy, they also sing**
> **(Ps 65:13).**

We know that angels are musical. God calls them **"morning stars"** and **"sons of God"** and makes reference to their singing as they were privileged to witness the creation of the world, **"when the morning stars sang together, and all the sons of God shouted for joy" (Job 38:7).** And at least one angel had built-in instruments to accompany his singing. We have reference to the creation of **"the anointed cherub" (Ez 28:14),** also known as Lucifer, who later fell and became God's enemy, Satan. In describing his original perfection and beauty, Ezekiel points out: **"the workmanship of thy tabrets and of thy pipes was prepared in thee in the day that thou wast created" (Ez 28:13).**

So at least this angel, who was the highest of all angels, was equipped with instruments as part of his angelic body. Perhaps others were similarly endowed.

Scripture reveals to us that God Himself sings: **". . . he will joy over thee with singing" (Zeph 3:17).** There is even reason to believe that our Lord may speak with a musical voice. The Apostle John testifies: **"I was in the Spirit on the Lord's day, and heard behind me a great voice, as of a trumpet, saying, I am Alpha and Omega, the first and the last" (Rev 1:11).**

Our God is a God of music, and He apparently takes such pleasure in music that He calls much of His creation, if not all of it, to make music. And of course, He calls man to make music to

Him as well. Man, the crown of creation, made in God's own image, after God's own likeness, has tremendous musical ability. Our creator made us with adroit fingers with which we are able to both manufacture and play a host of musical instruments. He made us with highly trainable and variable vocal chords, capable of an impressive range of pitch, volume, and resonant tone. He gave man the largest brain of any creature, capable of imagining, planning, and devising musical instruments, and composing a virtually unlimited assortment of musical expressions. From the native African beating out a simple rhythm on a hollow log, to the highly complex and sophisticated orchestral productions of Handel and Bach, man is the master of music among all of God's creatures.

Not only has God given man all the necessary tools with which to make pleasing music to Him, but our Creator also gave us a "heart" to govern our musical creativity. Though frequently misdirected to give praise and honor to anything and everything other than the Creator, man's heart is capable of **"love"** for his Creator, for the first and great command is:

> **Thou shalt love the Lord thy God with all thy heart, and
> with all thy soul, and with all thy strength, and with all thy
> mind" (Lk 10:27).**

Once the heart is appropriately directed to love the Creator with the whole being, God further commands us:

> **Praise ye the Lord. Sing unto the Lord a new song, and his
> praise in the congregation of saints...let them sing praises
> unto him with the timbrel and harp. For the Lord taketh
> pleasure in his people (Ps 149: 1-4).**

What a joy, to think that the God of the universe can find pleasure in His people who love Him! And one way that we can bring Him pleasure is to sing His praises with the voice that He gave us, and our fingers on the strings of a harp, and a host of other instruments, as Psalm 150 exhorts:

> **Praise ye the Lord. Praise God in his sanctuary: praise him
> in the firmament of his power. Praise him for his mighty
> acts: praise him according to his excellent greatness. Praise
> him with the sound of the trumpet: praise him with the
> psaltery and harp. Praise him with the timbrel and dance:
> praise him with stringed instruments and organs. Praise
> him upon the loud cymbals: praise him upon the high
> sounding cymbals. Let every thing that hath breath praise
> the Lord. Praise ye the Lord.**

4

Music in the Old Testament Temple

Listen. Can you hear it? The bleating of sheep, the snorting of bulls, the sizzling of roasting meat, the jingling of priests' bells, the dripping of blood in a basin—just a few of the sounds one would hear around the Old Testament temple. And, Oh! yes, the ever-present melody of a men's chorus singing praises to God.

The temple was God's dwelling place among His chosen people, the Israelites. Think of it! The God of the universe actually took up residence on earth, basically in a little box called the Ark of the Covenant. When it was first built the Ark was housed by a tent, or tabernacle, set up within a fenced-in area. The whole arrangement was carried about from place to place with the Hebrews while they wandered in the wilderness. They finally settled in the Promised Land and eventually built a temple to house the Ark on a more permanent basis.

The temple, being God's house, required much special treatment and maintenance. Different groups of Levitical priests were appointed to different jobs, and one group of priests was given a very special task, singing:

> **And these are the singers, chief of the fathers of the Levites,**
> **who remaining in the chambers were free: for they were**
> **employed in that work day and night (1 Chron 9:33).**

Notice that, it was not just anybody who was privileged to be a temple singer. That job was reserved for the **"chief of the fathers of the Levites,"** the most important men in the whole congregation of Israel. And it wasn't something they did in their spare time, you know, like a hobby, like playing golf or singing with a glee club after they got home from work. But singing was their full time employment, they had no other job. And they did it day and night. Their singing never stopped. They had a day shift and a night shift, 24 hours a day of continual singing in the temple chambers.

Of most importance, there was no audience of people listening to these men sing—God was their audience. This was no public performance, the singing in the Old Testament temple was exclusively for God's listening pleasure. We find the same occurrence in Ezekiel's vision of the future temple:

**And without the inner gate were the chambers of the singers
in the inner court . . . . (Eze 40:44).**

This should tell us something of God's love for music. Are you beginning to notice that wherever we find God, we find music? Wherever He takes up residence, music abounds. David cried:

O thou that inhabitest the praises of Israel (Ps 22:3).

God lives there, He camps out in the midst of music that brings glory to Him. What a privilege, what an honor you have as a musician, to be able to produce that thing called *music* which God so dearly loves. And for harpers, you can play His favorite instrument. His presence is surely with you.

5

MUSIC IN THE NEW TESTAMENT TEMPLE

Where does God live today? His portable, Old Testament house, the tabernacle, has been missing for centuries, so He doesn't live there any more. The grand temple that Solomon built for His dwelling place in Jerusalem was demolished long ago, so that's not His address either. And this may come as a surprise, but, contrary to popular belief, God does not take up residence in the church buildings of our land. We do greatly err to call our church buildings *"the house of the Lord,"* or *"God's house."* However, according to the Bible, God does have a house on earth to live in these days, a tabernacle or temple, and it happens to be your physical body:

> **What? Know ye not that your body is the temple of the Holy Ghost which is in you? (1 Cor 6:19).**

Just as God lived in an earthly temple among His people in Old Testament days, so He does today. But His present temple is your body. And just as He appointed priests to take care of maintenance and various duties in the Old Testament temple, as well as singing, so He has appointed priests to do all of that today. And guess who the priests are:

> **But ye are a chosen generation, a royal priesthood, an holy nation, a peculiar people; that ye should shew forth the praises of him who hath called you out of darkness into his marvellous light (1 Pet 2:9).**

If you are a Christian, you are a priest--indeed, a priest within a **"royal priesthood."** And one of the duties we are appointed to as priests is to **"shew forth the praises of him."** Therefore, He commands us in numerous places throughout the New Testament to sing and make music to Him:

> **Speaking to yourselves in psalms and hymns and spiritual songs, singing and making melody in your heart to the Lord (Eph 5:19).**

Why does God want the New Testament Christian to sing and make melody in the heart to Him? Obviously, for the same reason the Old Testament temple singers were commanded to do so, and for the same reason all of creation is commanded to do so, because it gives Him pleasure.

That's why He made it all in the first place, for His pleasure:

**Thou art worthy, O Lord, to receive glory and honour and
power: for thou hast created all things, and for thy pleasure
they are and were created (Rev 4:11).**

We exist for the purpose of giving Him pleasure, and one way we can do that is to fill His temple with the music that He loves, **"psalms, hymns, and spiritual songs, singing and making melody in your heart to the Lord."** And a deeper study of this verse in Ephesians will reveal something else of particular interest to anyone involved with harps. This word, **"melody,"** is translated from the Greek word, *"psallo,"* which, according to Vine's Expository Dictionary, happens to be defined as:

> primarily *"to twitch, twang,"* then, *"to play a stringed instrument with the
> fingers,"* and hence, in the Sept., *"to sing with a harp, sing psalms,"* denotes, in
> the NT, *"to sing a hymn, sing praise"* (Vine 402).

We find similar commands elsewhere in the New Testament, such as:

**Let the word of Christ dwell in you richly in all wisdom;
teaching and admonishing one another in psalms and hymns
and spiritual songs, singing with grace in your hearts to the
Lord (Col 3:16).**

Again, a careful study of this verse is most revealing. The word **"psalms"** is translated from the Greek, *"psalmos,"* which, according Vine's Expository Dictionary, means:

> primarily denoted *"a striking or twitching with the fingers
> (on musical strings)",* then, *"a sacred song, sung to musical
> accompaniment, a psalm"* (Vine 497).

It is significant that we, New Testament Christians, are instructed to sing Old Testament "psalms." In defining the word "psalm" the Wycliffe Bible Encyclopedia explains:

**The Gr. word "pslam" was used to translate the Heb. word
mizmor and probably means a song sung to the
accompaniment of stringed instruments" (Wycliffe 1423 – 1424).**

Since we are instructed to sing "psalms," which, by definition, involve the use of instruments, and many of the psalms themselves contain exhortations to use instruments, I conclude that it is not unreasonable to assume that God intended New Testament Christians to use instruments in worship. Let His New Testament temple be filled with the music He loves, as it was in the Old Testament, and as it is in Heaven, so let it be now, for His pleasure and His glory.

PART 2

Worship

6

THE HIGHEST CALLING

Jesus once visited two sisters: Mary and Martha. From all we can gather, based on the brief written account of this visit, it seems that these two ladies were quite typical sisters. We find them having somewhat of a scrap over the domestic duties that generally arise whenever company shows up. Diligent Martha busied herself taking care of every detail of housework, food preparation and serving to make sure everything was just the way it ought to be. But Mary took her leisure at Jesus' feet, intently listening to all He had to say, to the total neglect of cleaning, cooking, and serving. Now Martha was apparently upset that her sister should leave all the household duties to her, so she called on Jesus to instruct Mary about getting her priorities straight:

**Lord, dost thou not care that my sister hath left me to serve
alone? bid her therefore that she help me (Lk 10:40).**

To her surprise, Jesus does give corrective instruction, but not to Mary. Instead, Jesus replies:

**Martha, Martha, thou art careful and troubled about many
things; But one thing is needful: and Mary hath chosen that
good part, which shall not be taken away from her (Lk 10:41-42).**

In Jesus' view, **"that good part"** was to sit at His feet, bathe in His words, and worship Him.

There's a message here, folks, a message that each of us needs to hear, and hear well. Too often we tend to be *service* oriented, that is, we *serve* at the expense of *worship.* True, we each have our *calling* to some form of *service,* but sometimes that *service* becomes the most important thing in the world. Big sister Martha apparently felt her *calling* was hospitality. And like Martha, we can get so preoccupied with fulfilling our *calling* to *serve* that we neglect our *higher calling,* which is worship. Church responsibilities, duties in the home, on the job, in the community-- these are all wonderful avenues for serving. We all need a measure of involvement in service. The Lord expects us to serve, and indeed, commands us to, as *serving* is the fulfillment the golden rule, **". . . whatsoever ye would that men should do to you, do ye even so to them . . . . (Matt 7:12)."** Jesus phrased it a bit differently when he commanded, **". . . love thy neighbor as thyself" (Matt 22:39),** and that generally boils down to *serving* in its many forms. However, let's not forget that this commandment to **"love your neighbor as yourself"** is not the **"first and great command."** It is the **"second"** command, which is like the first, and perhaps an extension of the first, but it is not the first. The **"first and great command,"** as Jesus put it, is:

Thou shalt love the Lord thy God with all thy heart, and with all thy soul, and with all thy mind. This is the first and great commandment (Matt 22:37-38).

We see then that, as important as *serving* is, *worship* is more important still. Whatever our *calling* to service may be, let's remember the *highest calling,* as little sister Mary choose, **"that good part,"** to sit at Jesus' feet, bathe in His words, and worship Him.

7

A Closer Look at Worship

Going to church on Sunday to listen to a sermon does not necessarily constitute *"worship."* It is entirely possible to do all the things we typically do on the *"Lord's Day"* without ever actually worshipping. You can put money in the offering plate, but that does not mean you have worshipped. You can shake the preacher's hand, mouth the words of several hymns, head up the Bingo tournament for the building fund, and do all sorts of things that people do at church, but that still does not necessarily mean you have worshipped. You can even teach a Sunday school class, recite Bible verses, say prayers, play a hymn on an instrument, and take Holy Communion without ever actually worshipping. The simple reason is that *"worship"* does not necessarily consist of any outward act. There are many acts that *can be* acts of worship, but worship does not lie in the act, it lies in the heart.

The word *"worship"* is a fascinating word. Our English word comes from the Old English, *"worthship,"* and in the New Testament the Greek word that is typically translated **"worship"** is *"proskuneo."* Now this Greek word has two parts, the prefix, *"pros"* means *"to",* or *"toward,"* and the root word, *"kuneo"* literally means *"to kiss" (Vine 686)*. Doesn't that shed a lot of light on what *worship* is all about? It means to *"kiss toward."* Worship means to offer up *kisses of affection* to the one that we love with our whole heart, soul, mind and strength. That's what David was doing out on the mountain side while tending his sheep. He was offering up *kisses of affection* to his Creator, with his harp and voice:

> **. . . . unto thee will I sing with the harp, O thou Holy One of**
> **Israel. My lips shall greatly rejoice when I sing unto thee;**
> **and my soul, which thou hast redeemed. My tongue also**
> **shall talk of thy righteousness all the day long . . . . (Ps 71:22-24).**

A heart that rejoices in the beauty and awesomeness of its Creator-- that is what constitutes *worship*. Put that heart behind any act and it becomes an act of worship. But any act without a heart of worship behind it is just one more mundane ritual with zero spiritual merit. Backsliding Israel faithfully continued to carry out many required acts of worship, but look what God says:

> **. . . Forasmuch as this people draw near me with their**
> **mouth, and with their lips do honour me, but have removed**
> **their heart far from me . . . . (Is 29:13).**

Remember that our purpose for existence is to give God pleasure and glory, of which He receives none when *acts* of worship have no *heart* of worship behind them. May I encourage you, the musician, to play and sing from your heart. Think about the words of the songs you play and sing. Arrange your instrumental accompaniment such that it expresses the meaning of the words. Let your music be a *"kiss of affection"* from your heart to His.

> **It is a good thing to give thanks unto the Lord, and to sing praises unto thy name, O most High: To shew forth thy lovingkindness in the morning, and thy faithfulness every night. Upon an instrument of ten strings, and upon the psaltery; upon the harp with a solemn sound. For thou, Lord, hast made me glad through thy work: I will triumph in the works of thy hands. O Lord, how great are thy works! . . . (Ps 92:1-5).**

PART 3

Man's Pleasure
in Music

"SING ALOUD UNTO GOD OUR STRENGTH:
MAKE A JOYFUL NOISE UNTO THE GOD OF JACOB.
TAKE A PSALM, AND BRING HITHER THE TIMBREL,
THE PLEASANT HARP WITH THE PSALTRY"
(PS 81:1-2)

8

THE PLEASANT HARP

Sing aloud unto God our strength: make a joyful noise unto the God of Jacob. Take a psalm, and bring hither the timbrel, the pleasant harp with the psaltery. Blow up the trumpet in the new moon, in the time appointed, on our solemn feast day (Ps 81:1-2).

The psalmist mentions several different instruments here, but only the harp is referred to as **"pleasant."** This is not to say that other instruments are not pleasant, for indeed, they can be, but the harp is in focus here. Often, when someone is learning to play a new instrument they can make some rather "unpleasant" sounds. I'll never forget when my younger sister took up the violin in high school. Now, I don't know if you have ever heard a beginner on the violin, but my sister could cause pain. She used to practice in the living room, and of course the whole family would be sitting there, and the dog, Snoopy, would be lying on the floor. My sister would no sooner start to squeak and screech on that violin, and poor Snoopy would begin to moan, then he'd groan, then start to howl like a wolf. He spoke for us all. My sister's heart was in the right place, she was doing the best she could, but, Oh!--the pain. A lot of instruments can be like that, but a harp always sounds pleasant. Even if it's a beginner playing, even if a two-year old just starts yanking on the strings, a harp always makes a pleasant sound. In fact, the only time I have ever heard a harp make an unpleasant sound was when one fell over and crashed on the floor. Now to a harp-maker, that is a terrifying sound, but other than that, they always sound pleasant.

As a family we go a lot of places with our harps. It is with fond memories that I recall our first public exposure, the homeschool curriculum fair in Harrisburg. Thousands of people milled around looking tired and dazed as they waded through an ocean of curriculum booths trying to figure out which math book to buy for their second grader. Time and again people would stroll past our booth, stop abruptly, and stare. The fatigued, dazed look on their faces evolved into a blend of pleasant interest, wonder, and amazement, as they melted into a state of euphoric tranquility. Speechless for a time, they'd linger, basking in the heavenly strains that flowed from the harps as our daughters played. Then they would start groping for words, and most everyone seemed to arrive at the same verbal expression to describe this unexpected phenomena—"beauuuuuuuuuuuuutiful!"

We sold a lot of recordings that day, and even a harp. This being our first public appearance we had been feeling somewhat unsure about what kind of response we would receive, but the comments were so encouraging. People said things like, "Your booth is like an oasis in the Sahara Desert." "I could stay here for hours." "This is such a blessing." "If we buy a harp do the girls come with it?" We seemed to have a crowd around our booth all day. Even the other vendors at the booths near us came over and thanked us for setting up our booth near them as they were so blessed by the soothing music on such a stressful day. Some even made special request with the management to have their booth placed next to ours at next year's fair.

I share all this not to boast, but simply to encourage you as a musician, and particularly, you as a harper. As always, the Bible proves itself to be true. Few would argue with its reference to the harp as **"pleasant."** Indeed, the harp is pleasant to God, and pleasant to people, and you, the harper, have the marvelous privilege of providing pleasant music for both God and man to enjoy.

9

THE BLESSING OF BEING A BLESSING

Blessing – noun 1. That which makes happy or prosperous
(Funk & Wagnalls 146).

Abraham proved his faith in God by demonstrating his willingness to offer up his only son, Isaac, at the Lord's command. You know the story. Even as Abraham was about to slay his son as an offering, God stopped him and provided a ram in place of Isaac, so that Isaac could be saved. It was just a test, and God was so pleased with Abraham's faithful obedience that He bestowed a two-fold blessing upon the man:

> **. . . in blessing I will bless thee, and in multiplying I will**
> **multiply thy seed as the stars of the heaven, and as the sand**
> **which is upon the sea shore; and thy seed shall possess the**
> **gate of his enemies (Gen 22:17).**

That is the first part of the blessing. Good things were in store for Abraham and his descendents. But beyond that, God adds a wonderful extension to this blessing:

> **And in thy seed shall all the nations of the earth be blessed**
> **(Gen 22:18).**

Here is the second part of the blessing. Not only would Abraham and his descendents be blessed, but they would also **"be"** a blessing to others, even to all the nations of the earth. It's a great thing to receive a blessing from God, but it's an even greater thing to be used by God to **"be"** a blessing to others. For Abraham, the primary fulfillment of this *blessing of being a blessing* came centuries later when one of his descendents would actually be the Christ of God. What an honor God gave to Abraham, to have his lineage culminate in the Lord's Messiah, who would save His people from their sins! God provided His Son, Jesus, the Lamb of God, of the seed of Abraham, an offering on the cross in place of sinners who deserved to die for their sins, so that sinners could be saved. And not only would this salvation be offered to the nation of Israel, but it would be extended to all nations of the earth. Think of it! Even we Gentiles from every tribe and tongue and people and nation have the incredible privilege of being grafted into Abraham's lineage. What a blessing God has granted to us, through father Abraham and his descendents! Indeed, all the nations of the earth are blessed in Abraham, and to this very day Abraham is enjoying the *blessing of being a blessing* to all nations of the earth.

One of the wondrous things about Abraham's blessing is the way it proliferates. Each of us can have a very real part in Abraham's two-fold blessing, especially those who play an instrument and/or sing. Maybe we won't have as many descendents as Abraham, but we can still **"be"** a blessing to many. If you have ever played or sung for people you have likely been told that your music is *"a blessing."* Now think about that. Isn't it a blessing to be able to **"be"** a blessing to others? Just because music is so pleasant to the ears of mankind, you can be a blessing just by playing and singing. But beyond that, if you are a Christian, you are, spiritually, of the seed of Abraham, and therefore, partaker of the blessed promises made to him. And if you play and sing sacred music that honors God and His Christ, you are helping to proliferate the blessing. When you communicate the Gospel message through music you plant seeds of faith in unbelievers, and you strengthen the faith of believers. You are therefore further blessed by being a blessing to others. Isn't that a blessing? Go therefore, and bless others with your music, and be blessed.

PART 4

Harps in the Bible

10

TO HARP OR NOT TO HARP
(PART 1)

> **To every thing there is a season, and a time to every purpose
> under the heaven: A time to be born, and a time to die; a
> time to plant, and a time to pluck up that which is planted;
> A time to kill, and a time to heal; A time to . . . .
> (Ecc 2:1-3).**

On the passage goes listing quite a few **"things"** that have their **"season,"** that appropriate time to be done, and not to be done. Though the Preacher of Ecclesiastes does not list *"harping,"* or the playing of other instruments in this particular passage, this too is one of those **"purposes under the heaven"** that has its season. There is a time to harp, or play other instruments, and a time not to harp, or play other instruments.

We find throughout the Bible the harp being mentioned some 51 times. There seems to be a certain set of circumstances or **"seasons"** that call for the harp and other instruments to be heard. Likewise, there are other **"seasons"** that call for their silence. At seasons of rejoicing, celebrating, important turns of events, fervent worship and thanksgiving, these are times when the harp and other instruments seem to be a must in the Bible. Here are a few examples:

- In 1 Sam 10:1-6 Saul was anointed the first king of Israel. He received the Spirit of the Lord, and he was turned into another man. Present at the celebration were the psaltery, tabret, pipe, and harp.

- As king, Saul disobeyed God once too often. He was rejected as king; the Spirit of the Lord departed from him; and the Bible says **". . . an evil spirit from the Lord troubled him" (1 Sam 16:14).** The remedy? **". . . David took an harp, and played with his hand: so Saul was refreshed, and was well, and the evil spirit departed from him (1 Sam 16:23).** It was the season for the harp.

- In 1 Chron 15:28 the ark of the covenant, (God's presence and dwelling place) had been in someone else's possession for a long time. David fetched it and carried it back to reside in Jerusalem where it belonged. What a celebration took place on that day! Shouting, dancing, lots of instruments, one of which was, of course, the harp.

- In 2 Chron 5:6-14 King Solomon spent years building a grand temple to house the ark of the covenant. When it was finally completed the ark was carried into the temple with great rejoicing, singing, and instrument playing. One of the instruments played was the harp. And God responded to all the praising and thanksgiving by filling the house with a cloud, the Shekinah glory.

- Instruments were present at the celebration when God caused the enemies of Jehoshaphat to destroy one another so that Judah didn't even have to fight. **". . . for the Lord had made them rejoice…and they came to Jerusalem with psalteries and harps and trumpets unto the house of the Lord" (2 Chron 20:27-28).**

- Israel had failed to follow God for a long time. After much warning, God chastened them by allowing their nation to be destroyed. The grand temple was demolished, the mighty wall around Jerusalem was rubble, and the people were exiled. After a lengthy and sad time in exile, and much repentance, God arranged for Nehemiah to return to Jerusalem with a group of workers to rebuild the wall. How they rejoiced when it was finished.! A dedication ceremony was held, and everybody came **"with gladness, both with thanksgivings, and with singing, with cymbals, psalteries, and with harps" (Neh 12:27). "For God made them rejoice with great joy" (Neh 12:43).**

- Throughout the Psalms David praised God with the harp and other instruments for His great works. Many times instruments play an integral role in worship such as we find in Psalm 33: **"Rejoice in the Lord, O ye righteous: for praise is comely for the upright. Praise the Lord with harp; sing unto him with the psaltery and an instrument of ten strings. Sing unto him a new song; play skillfully with a loud noise" (Ps 33:1-3).**

- Heaven is the place of eternal rejoicing where there is no tear to be found. The apostle John had the incredible privilege of being taken up to heaven, and what do you suppose he heard up there? **"And I heard the voice of harpers harping with their harps" (Rev 14:2).**

- Heaven is the place of eternal victory over sin and all evil. While in heaven, John's eyes were dazzled by a sight located directly in front of God's throne: **". . . a sea of glass mingled with fire: and them that had gotten the victory over the beast, and over his image, and over his mark, and over the number of his name, stand on the sea of glass, having the harps of God" (Rev 15:2).**

- Heaven is the place of eternal worship and thanksgiving. John had the awesome opportunity to view God's very throne, and don't you know what he saw round about God's very throne? **". . . the four beasts and four and twenty elders fell down before the Lamb, having every one of them harps . . . ." (Rev 5:8).**

During this life, at a time of rejoicing, celebrating, a great turn of events, a time of fervent worship and thanksgiving, this is the time to harp and play other instruments. It is the **"season"** when it is appropriate. But what a future we have in heaven, for heaven is the place of the *eternal* **"season"** of the harp.

These are the times not to harp or play other instruments: times of judgment, chastening, destruction, sorrow, mourning and weeping. A silent harp is a sign that things are not well; there is no joy, no hope, no favor with God.

King David experienced times of hopelessness. He speaks of them in the Psalms:

> **Judge me, O God, and plead my cause against an ungodly**
> **nation: O deliver me from the deceitful and unjust man. For**
> **thou art the God of my strength: why go I mourning because**
> **of the oppression of the enemy? (Ps 43:1-2).**

Things are not well with David right now. Notice all the negative words here: judgment, pleading, ungodly, deceitful, unjust, mourning, oppression, enemies. But after this negative beginning David then looks on the bright side and the whole attitude changes:

> **"O send out thy light and thy truth: let them lead me,**
> **let them bring me unto thy holy**
> **hill and to thy tabernacles" (Ps 43:3).**

Now notice all the positive words: light, truth, God's leading, God's holy hill, God's tabernacles. And now that he is oriented on the positive side of things, note the result:

> **Then will I go unto the altar of God, unto God my exceeding**
> **joy: yea, upon the harp will I praise thee, O God my God**
> **(Ps 43:4).**

This is the season for the harp. Things are well again. He is at the altar of God, his exceeding joy. What else can he do now but praise. David even challenges himself as to why he was ever negative in the first place:

> **Why art thou cast down, O my soul? And why art thou**
> **disquieted within me? Hope in God: for I shall yet praise**
> **him, who is the health of my countenance, and my God (Ps 43:5).**

To harp or not to harp? That is the question. And it all depends on our relationship with God. In hopeless despair, when the heart is hard and unrepentant, faithless, in disfavor with God—hang it up. But when we are right with God, and all is well, faith has risen, and hope lives:

> **. . . I will sing and give praise. Awake up, my glory; awake,**
> **psaltery and harp . . . . (Ps 57:7-8).**

12

EVIL SPIRITS AND HARPS

Everywhere I go, when people discover that I'm involved with harps, one of the first things they will often mention is the story of David playing the harp for King Saul when he was troubled by an evil spirit. It's an intriguing story. However, the whole story is usually not told, leaving people to draw all sorts in inaccurate conclusions about music, harps, evil spirits, and troubled people. Some may even conclude that the harp has the power to exorcise (cast out) demon spirits. Let's get a bit of background first and then see if we can't paint a complete picture to base our conclusions on.

The Story: Saul had a good start as the first king of Israel. He was chosen by God Himself and anointed by the prophet, Samuel, who told him:

> **. . . thou shalt come to the hill of God . . . thou shalt meet a**
> **company of prophets coming down from the high place with**
> **a psaltery, and a tabret, and a pipe, and a harp . . . and they**
> **shall prophesy. And the Spirit of the Lord will come upon**
> **thee, and thou shalt prophesy with them, and shalt be turned**
> **into another man (1 Sam 10:5-6).**

Samuel also told Saul: **"God is with thee" (1 Sam 10:7).** When Samuel finished speaking with Saul the Bible says: **". . . God gave him another heart: and all those signs came to pass that day" (1 Sam 10:9).** So the harp was present when the Spirit of the Lord came upon Saul and turned him into a new man with a new heart. And things went well for Saul as he started out doing things God's way, while he was **"little" (1 Sam 15:17)** in his own sight. But pride got the best of him, and as time went on Saul disobeyed God once too often, taking liberties beyond his bounds. It became evident that he was bent on doing things his own way rather than God's way. Therefore God rejected Saul as king. In his place a young, handsome fellow named David was anointed to be King over Israel:

> **. . . and the Spirit of the Lord came upon David from that**
> **day forward . . . but the Spirit of the Lord departed from**
> **Saul, and an evil spirit from the Lord troubled him" (1 Sam 16:13).**

It must have been rather disturbing for Saul's servants to have a king who was troubled by an evil spirit, so they put their heads together and came up with a solution:

> **Let our lord now command thy servants . . . to seek out a**
> **man, who is a cunning player on an harp: and it shall come**

**to pass, when the evil spirit from God is upon thee, that he
shall play with his hand, and thou shalt be well (1 Sam
16:16).**

Saul agreed to the plan. And one of the servants happened to know that David was just such a
"cunning player," so he was called from tending his sheep:

> **And David came to Saul, and stood before him: and he loved
> him greatly; and he became his armourbearer . . . And it
> came to pass, when the evil spirit from God was upon Saul,
> that David took an harp, and played with his hand, so Saul
> was refreshed, and was well, and the evil spirit departed
> from him (1 Sam 16:21-23).**

This is where the story usually ends whenever people make reference to David playing
his harp for Saul. Conclusions are drawn, opinions are fixed, and various claims are made about
certain kinds of music, harps, evil spirits, and troubled people. But this is not the end of the story.

The Rest of the Story: First and foremost, it is important to note that at this point in the story things
were good between Saul and David. Saul even **"loved him greatly."** This is significant, because
it was only during this time of good relations between Saul and David that David's harp playing
brought relief from the troubling evil spirit. And apparently there were numerous occasions when
David used the harp to drive away that troubling evil spirit.

But then things changed, and jealousy ruined their relationship. It all revolved around the
episode with Goliath. You know the story. This big fellow from Gath came, ridiculing, threatening,
and challenging Israel. And the boy, little David, stood right up to his face and took him on. All the
other men in Israel cowered back, shaking in their boots. And understandably so. Goliath was a big
man--over nine feet tall--and a seasoned warrior. But young David dropped him with one stone in
his sling, and then lopped off his head with Goliath's own sword. The whole Philistine army ran
for it, and Israel's army pursued and slaughtered countless Philistines. It was a tremendous victory,
and Saul was so impressed with David that he set him over the men of war. Everything was looking
up, until that fateful day when Saul led his army back home:

> **. . . the women came out of all cities of Israel, singing and
> dancing, to meet king Saul . . . and said, Saul hath slain his
> thousands, and David his ten thousands" (1 Sam 18:6-7).**

That was the end of Saul's relationship with David.

> **And Saul was very wroth, and the saying displeased him;
> and he said, They have ascribed unto David ten thousands,
> and to me they have ascribed but thousands: and what can**

**he have more but the kingdom? And Saul eyed David from
that day forward (1 Sam 18:8-9).**

Not only was this the end of Saul's relationship with David, but no more would David's cunning harp playing bring relief to Saul:

**And it came to pass on the morrow, that the evil spirit from
God came upon Saul . . . and David played with his hand, as
at other times, and there was a javelin in Saul's hand. And
Saul cast the javelin; for he said, I will smite David even to
the wall with it. And David avoided out of his presence twice
(1 Sam 18:10-11).**

The same thing happened again a short time later. Saul was troubled by the evil spirit, David played the harp, and Saul, in an angry rage of jealousy, tried to pin him to the wall with his javelin. This time David fled, knowing that Saul had it in for him. And Saul spent the rest of his life hunting David down and trying to kill him.

The Lesson: Many spiritual lessons can be drawn out of this story, but the one in focus here as pertains to harps is to be aware of the limitations of the harp. Yes, David's harp playing did drive away Saul's troubling evil spirit--at least, sometimes, and under certain conditions. So perhaps the harp has some power over evil spirits, at least, when played by a Godly person like David on whom the Spirit of the Lord rested, and under the right conditions. But human will and emotions enter the picture too. Saul set his will to kill David, and his will, anger and jealousy remained unaffected by David's harp playing. So be careful, harper. The interaction of the spiritual realm with human will and emotions is very mysterious leaving many questions unanswered. Be careful about trying to cast a demon out of somebody by playing your harp, especially if they happen to have a javelin in their hand and have anger or jealousy toward you. And be aware that the harp was never used anywhere else in the Bible to cast a demon out. In the New Testament particularly, it was always done simply by speaking. And Jesus also brought out the necessity of fasting and prayer for exorcising certain kinds of demons.

Now it is true that the harp can have a relaxing, soothing, calming affect on people who are stressed out, but that is very different from the situation with Saul. So be careful about the conclusions that people draw from this story, because most times such conclusions do not take into account the whole story.

13

TO MEDITATE WITH HARPS

As the Bible uses the word **"meditate"** it generally carries the idea of *deep thinking.* Some of the original words that are translated **"meditate"** would literally mean *"to speak with oneself," "to mutter," "to meditate on divine things" (Wycliffe 1095).* There is a very real and necessary place for this activity of **"meditation"** in everybody's life. The psalmists did a lot of it. In fact the entire Book of Psalms is a collection of such **"meditations,"** or deep thoughts, taking various forms such as songs, hymns, poems, and prayers. And interestingly, the harp played an integral role in the meditation process. In fact, the Psalms were generally intended to be sung to the accompaniment of a stringed instrument, and primarily, the harp. Numerous psalms mention the harp specifically, and sometimes the harp is directly associated with meditation:

> **My mouth shall speak of wisdom: and the meditation of my
> heart shall be of understanding. I will incline mine ear to a
> parable: I will open my dark saying upon the harp (Ps 49:3-4).**

Now, I can't play the harp, so I cannot speak from experience here, but as I watch people play it surely seems to me that a person could play very meditatively--that is, putting a psalm or some passage of Scripture to music, and playing it, singing it, and musing over the meaning of the words. It seems that a harper could express the meaning of the words by the very melody he plays by finding just that appropriate tune, pitch, tempo, beat, and volume that would carry and express the message behind the words. It seems like a person really could **"open a dark saying upon the harp,"** a **"dark saying"** perhaps referring to a passage that might be difficult to understand.

This idea of harp-assisted meditation in the psalms is further brought out by the use of the word **"Selah."** Throughout the psalms we find this word appearing over 70 times. **"Selah"** is a Hebrew word that means **"an intended pause either in the singing of the psalm or in the instrumental accompaniment" (Wycliffe 1546).** **"Selah"** indicates a pause, or musical or instrumental interlude where the psalmist would stop and mediate on the words he just spoke or sang while playing instrumentally. The interlude could be just a few notes, or an extended period of instrumental playing.

In Psalm 32 the word **"Selah"** appears three different times. This psalm was written by King David, no doubt after his sin of adultery. In the first part of the psalm we find David expressing his experience of first trying to hide his sin and cover it up:

> **When I kept silence, my bones waxed old through my
> roaring all the day long. For day and night thy hand was**

> **heavy upon me: my moisture is turned into the drought of**
> **summer. Selah (Ps 32:3-4).**

At this point in the psalm the word **"Selah"** tells us that David paused here from any further words, and he played a melody that expressed what he was feeling right here—you know, that awful, dry, painful burden of shame and guilt that he had been carrying for so long while trying to hide his sin. Perhaps you can relate to that. I certainly can. And David just muses and meditates over the weightiness and grief of his sin, and how it gave him no peace, no rest. Day and night he could feel God's hand heavy upon him while his conscience was **"roaring"** at him. And then, after his period of meditation, David proceeds:

> **I acknowledged my sin unto thee, and mine iniquity have I**
> **not hid. I said, I will confess my transgressions unto the**
> **Lord: and thou forgavest the iniquity of my sin. Selah (Ps 32:5).**

After wrestling for so long over this sin David finally realizes there is only one thing he can do-- nothing else can take care of his guilt--nothing else can bring him the peace that he once knew. He finally faces his only recourse—to acknowledge his sin and stop hiding it:

> **I will confess my transgressions unto the Lord: and thou**
> **forgavest the iniquity of my sin. Selah.**

Again, **"Selah"** tells us that David paused here from any further words, and he played a melody that expressed what he was feeling right here in this climax of finally facing truth, and making an honest, open confession of his sin. With no excuses, no justification, no blame-shifting, David simply owns his own guilt. He casts himself before the mercy seat of God, and he experienced the forgiveness of God:

> **. . . thou forgavest the iniquity of my sin. Selah.**

That's what he stopped to meditate on--that relief, that release, that cleansing, that healing, and all the feelings that go along with it. Enough with the words! Words just could not really say it. So he stopped to meditate, and express that emotional climax with a wordless melody that fit the occasion.

In our Christian hymns I'm afraid we have gotten away from making use of **"Selah."** These days we just sing one verse after the other, and there is no place in there to pause, ponder, and meditate. Let's bring it back, musician. Let's incorporate **"Selah"** back into Godly music, and include those thought-provoking, experience- expressing instrumental interludes that are skillfully arranged to foster meditation.

PART 5

Spiritual Gifts

"AND JESUS, WHEN HE WAS BAPTIZED,
WENT UP STRAIGHTWAY OUT OF THE WATER:
AND, LO, THE HEAVENS WERE OPENED UNTO HIM,
AND HE SAW THE SPIRIT OF GOD DESCENDING LIKE A DOVE,
AND LIGHTING UPON HIM"
(MATT 3:16)

14

THE SPIRIT/HARP CONNECTION

This section of the Devotional Guide focuses on Spiritual gifts. Though harp playing, or any type of musicianship, is never specifically listed in the Bible as a "spiritual gift," it does have a place among the gifts. Indeed, harp playing is not only a spiritual gift, but can also be a manifestation of being "filled with the Spirit." Let's consider the connection between the harp and the Spirit:

> **And be not drunk with wine, wherein is excess; but be filled**
> **with the Spirit; speaking to yourselves in psalms and hymns**
> **and spiritual songs, singing and making melody in your**
> **heart to the Lord (Eph 5:19).**

We have here some instructions written by the Apostle Paul to the church in Ephesus. It is likely that there were some in this young church who had a problem with over-indulgence with alcohol, perhaps even attending church services a bit tipsy, resulting in some rather inappropriate behavior. So Paul gently attempts to clarify their thinking. The wording here seems to suggest that just as drunkenness is a manifestation of being filled with alcoholic spirits, similarly, **"singing and making melody in your heart to the Lord"** is a manifestation of being filled with the Holy Spirit of God. Just as there is a direct connection between the filling of alcoholic spirits and certain behaviors such as slurred speech, a staggering gate, and general uninhibited activity, so there is a direct connection between the filling tof the Holy Spirit and **"singing and making melody in your heart."** Let's look more closely at these important words **"singing and making melody."**

The word "singing" is translated from the Greek word, "adontes," which is derived from the root word, "ado," which, according to Vine's Expository Dictionary, "is used always of 'praise to God'" (Vine 578). So I think we can safely say that the singing of sacred music from the heart is a manifestation of the Holy Spirit of God, since "ado" always refers to singing "praise to God." On the other hand, the singing of non-sacred music that does not praise God is not a manifestation of the Holy Spirit, although it may well be a manifestation some other spirit or spirits, such as we might find in a bar room. Get the contrast? Filling with bar-room "spirits" produces bar-room singing, while filling with the Holy Spirit produces Holy Spirit singing.

The word "melody" is translated from the Greek word, "psallo," which means, "primarily, 'to twitch, twang,' then, 'to play a stringed instrument with the fingers,' and hence, in the Sept., 'to sing with a harp, sing psalms,' denotes in the NT, 'to sing a hymn, sing praise'" (Vine 402). So then, to "make melody" refers to singing sacred music while playing a harp, and this behavior is a manifestation of being filled with the Holy Spirit of God.

This connection between being **"filled with the Spirit"** and **"making melody"** (singing sacred music while playing the harp) is important to keep in mind as we consider the place of the harp and other instruments, and singing, among the spiritual gifts. This is not to suggest that every time anyone sings or plays sacred music on an instrument he is manifesting the filling of the Holy Spirit of God, but it can be so.

We find this connection in the Old Testament as well. Elisha had a double portion of Elijah's spirit. During his discussion with King Jehoshaphat, Elisha said: **"But now bring me a minstrel. And it came to pass, when the minstrel played, that the hand of the Lord came upon him. And he said, Thus saith the Lord.... (2 Kings 3:15-16)**. Elisha went on to prophesy concerning Jehoshaphat's future. But notice that it was the playing of the minstrel (on a stringed instrument) that brought the hand of the Lord upon Elisha, and he was empowered to manifest the spiritual gift of prophecy. Again, this does not suggest that every time anyone plays an instrument the hand of the Lord will come to manifest the gift of prohecy. But mysteriously, there is a connection at least some times, and every musician ought to be aware of it.

15

THE NATURE OF SPIRITUAL GIFTS

For quite some time in Christian circles much attention has been drawn to the gifts of the Spirit, through what has been called "The Charismatic Movement." Spiritual gifts are crucial to the stability and growth of the body of Christ, but the gifts need to be exercised with the proper goals in mind, and with the proper understanding of what they are. These matters are spelled out in various passages in the New Testament, and a look at the original language of these texts will shed great light on the subject. So brace yourself for a crash-course in Greek as we seek to understand spiritual gifts and the musician's place among them.

At creation God made man **"in his own image" (Gen 1:27).** He made us a lot like Himself, giving each of us a measure of His own character, His nature, His abilities, and His qualities. We are a finite representation of the infinite God. And though we all have similarities, He made each of us different, giving, by His Spirit, an extra measure of certain qualities and abilities to some that He did not give to others. So we call that extra measure a **"gift."** This idea comes out in the verse:

Now there are diversities of gifts, but the same Spirit (1 Cor 12:4).

The word **"diversities"** is a very important word here. When we think of **"diversities"** we generally think of things that are simply different, not the same. And that is part of the meaning here, but there is much more. **"Diversities"** is translated from the Greek word *"diairesis,"* which is a two part word. The prefix, *"dia"* means *"apart,"* and the root word, *"haireo,"* means *"to take"(Vine 168).* So this word literally means *"to take apart."* **"Diversities"** has to do with dividing, taking something whole and then separating it into individual elements or components or categories. Think of it as if the characteristics and qualities of the Godhead were separated or taken apart, and the pieces distributed to different members in the church. Those pieces, in English, are called **"gifts."**

When we think of **"gifts"** we generally think of something given, and that is part of the meaning in reference to **"diversities of gifts,"** but there is much more. The word **"gifts"** is translated from the Greek word *"charisma" (Vine 264).* This is the word behind the expression, The "Charismatic" Movement. The root word, *"charis,"* and its derivatives, are widely used throughout the New Testament, and they carry many shades of meaning. Interestingly, most of the time, *"charis"* is translated **"grace."** So both words, **"gifts"** and **"grace,"** are translated from the same Greek word, *"charis."*

Now the word **"grace"** has a number meanings, depending on the context in which it is used. But as pertains to the spiritual gifts we might think of them as *"gifts of grace" (Vine 264)*. A derivative of the same root word, *"charis"* is used to describe Jesus when He took human form:

> **And the Word was made flesh, and dwelt among us, (and we
> beheld his glory, the glory as of the only begotten of the
> Father) full of grace and truth (Jn 1:14).**

Jesus was full of **"grace and truth."** We often think of **"grace"** as meaning "unmerited favor," and it often does mean that. But not here. Jesus was not full of "unmerited favor." As used here, the context indicates that "grace" (from "charitos") refers to God-like qualities and abilities. We might speak of a person as being a very "gracious" person. What do we mean by that? We mean that a gracious person has God-like characteristics, as Jesus did. "The word was made flesh, and dwelt among us, (and we beheld his glory, the glory as of the only begotten of the Father)." What did we behold? His "glory," His God-likeness. We beheld that He was "full of grace and truth;" He was full of God-like qualities and abilities. Elsewhere Jesus is described as ". . . the brightness of His glory, the express image of His person . . . ." (Heb 1:3). "For in him dwelleth all the fullness of the Godhead bodily"(Col 2:9). All the God-like qualities and abilities that God has were present in Jesus. He was indeed God in the flesh. I think it is safe to say that Jesus possessed all of the spiritual gifts (graces), since "all the fullness of the Godhead" dwelled in Him. Consider the list of spiritual gifts given in 1 Corinthians 12:

> **gifts of administrations, operations, word of wisdom, word
> of knowledge, faith, healing, working of miracles, prophecy,
> discerning of spirits, tongues, interpretation of tongues,
> apostleship, teaching, helps, governments**

Doesn't that sound like Jesus? Isn't that what He is all about? This list of spiritual gifts is just a list of Jesus' qualities, characteristics, and abilities, most of which He exhibited while on the earth for all the world to see. But the day came when Jesus left this earth and ascended up to heaven. What God-likeness was then left for the world to see? Well, this is where the gifts come in. It's as if God took that **"fullness of the Godhead"** that dwelled in Jesus, and took it apart, separating it into diverse pieces. And by His Spirit He distributed those pieces (gifts) to the different members that make up the church. The church happens to be called **"the body of Christ"** because the church is now the manifestation of God-likeness in the world today. This is what spiritual gifts are all about. Each of us has an extra measure of one or more "graces" (God-like qualities and abilities) that God intends for us to exercise to bring stability and growth to His body on the earth. And be assured, musicianship has its place in all of that as we shall see.

16

Listed and Unlisted Gifts

In the Old Testament God specifically mentions men who were given a special artistic ability for building and ornamenting the tabernacle and its furnishings:

Bezaleel . . . I have filled him with the spirit of God, in wisdom, and in understanding, and in knowledge and in all manner of workmanship, to devise cunning works . . . And I, behold, I have given with him Aholiab . . . and in the hearts of all that are wise hearted I have put wisdom, that they may make all that I have commanded thee (Ex 31:2-6).

Although the special, artistic ability of these men to fabricate and ornament is not referred to as a "spiritual gift" in those exact terms, still, the description given here puts it in the category of "spiritual gifts." In order for Bezaleel (and the others) to have this special, artistic ability, God **"filled him with the spirit of God."** Therefore, their artistic gifts were indeed "spiritual gifts" even though we do not find such gifts specifically listed in any of the Biblical lists of gifts. And even though these gifts were given in Old Testament times, God still grants such gifts today. Perhaps you have seen some of the art work of Thomas Kinkade, painter of light. This fellow has the uncommon ability to paint beautiful scenes that appear to contain light. He typically quotes a Bible verse on his paintings that relates somehow to the scene he has painted. Many of us find the warmth and serenity of Kinkade's art work absolutely captivating, breath-taking. To gaze at his painting causes our faith to be strengthened and evokes love and worship of our Creator. It leaves us in awe that God gave a man the ability to capture light with paint and put it on canvas in an image, a likeness, of something in God's creation. How can he do it? Not just anybody can paint like that. Few would argue that Brother Kinkade is a "gifted" painter. God gave him a special ability to do something that most us cannot do.

Of course, I could paint a picture too. And when I'm finished you might even be able to tell what it's supposed to be. But the impact of my painting would be a far cry from that of Brother Kinkade, because he is a "gifted" painter, and I am not. Kinkade's artistic ability is substantially above that of the rest of us, we'd almost call it superhuman. But you know, as marvelous an artist as Brother Kinkade is, God is the ultimate artist. He dazzles us all day every day with sunrises, sunsets, blue skies with white puffy clouds, flowers, trees, mountains, canyons, oceans, rubies, emeralds, diamonds, peacocks, stars, galaxies, etc., etc., etc. And when He formed us in the womb in His own image, God took a small measure of His own artistic ability and put it within us. And by His Spirit, He put within Thomas Kinkade an extra measure of His own artistic ability. This is the nature of spiritual gifts. They are God-like qualities and abilities that, by His Spirit, God puts within us, the ones He made in His own image.

Now "painting" is not specifically listed as a "spiritual gift" in any of the Biblical lists, but it is none-the-less a gift. Indeed, there are many gifts that are not specifically listed in the Bible as "gifts." Take hymn writing, for example. For centuries hymns have strengthened the faith of believers, and inspired us to love and worship. Most of us would have a hard time writing a hymn. But God gave special abilities to people like Isaac Watts, the Wesley brothers, and Fanny Crosby. These saints composed hymn after hymn that to this day still edify the body of Christ. But this ability to write beautiful, inspiring words of truth is just a small measure of God's own ability to express truth with beautiful inspiring words and tones. After all, he authored the whole Bible, ultimately, and inspired holy men to pen the words. What could be more inspiring than the Bible? And the original languages He used, both Hebrew and Greek, were musical or tonal languages in their day. There is even some Scripture that suggests that God Himself may speak with a musical voice. And the psalms are God's hymns. God was the first hymn writer. He holds the ultimate ability to write hymns. But He gave a measure of that ability to certain individuals to do what He does, and it is an ability that He did not give to the rest of us.

Of course, anyone can write a song. Even I wrote one. But alas, the song I authored did not make it to any list of top 10 greatest hits, and it was not considered for inclusion in any hymnal. Not a great many people were particularly impressed with it. Few had their faith strengthened by it, and few were moved to love and worship by it, because it was not the work of a gifted hymn writer. So it is with spiritual gifts, whether they are specifically listed in the Bible or not. The church will recognize the presence of a gift, or its absence. But just because we may lack this gift or that, we have no reason to be discouraged, because everyone has some gifts, and no one has all the gifts. That is why we are called to be part of a body, the body of Christ. And by working together in harmony as a united body, the church of Jesus Christ moves and accomplishes the work of God on the earth. As each member exercises his gifts, the special God-like qualities and abilities that God has given, God's kingdom is built. And that includes the special musical abilities that God has given to you. So, if you are a "gifted" musician, count yourself blessed. Count yourself endowed from on high with a very special "grace."

17

THE PURPOSE OF THE GIFTS

Most of the time when we are given a gift we view the gift as our own possession. We presume it was given to us for our own pleasure and benefit. And sometimes we like to show it off. Perhaps you have seen a young lady who has just been given a large diamond ring by her fiance. She embraces it as her own, and she's likely to be somewhat proud of it. She delights in flashing it around for all to see, fully expecting that others will be favorably impressed. Now that kind of behavior may be acceptable for a young bride-to-be, after all, the gift was given to her for her benefit. But not so when it comes to spiritual gifts. All of our thinking about "gifts" and their purpose must be completely rearranged. In the midst of his discussion on spiritual gifts, the Apostle Paul informs us:

> **But the manifestation of the Spirit is given to every man to profit withal (1 Cor 12:7).**

This statement tells us that God does not give gifts of grace for the benefit of the recipient of the gift, rather, it is for everybody's benefit. God does not give someone the gift of **"the word of wisdom"** just so he can enjoy having the word of wisdom for himself, and pridefully show off with it. God gives that gift so the recipient can bless others with it. God does not give somebody the gift of **"helps"** just so he can enjoy helping himself, but it is to help others. Gifts are given for everybody's profit, as Paul puts it, **"to profit withal,"** but there is more to this than meets the eye. **"Profit withal"** is translated from the Greek, *"sumpheron,"* which is a two-part word. The prefix, *"sum,"* means *"together with one another,"* and the root word, *"pheron"* means *"to bring or to carry."* So literally, *"sumpheron"* means *"to bring together."* This is the purpose of spiritual gifts, they are intended to bring Christians together to a loving oneness, an interdependent united body. Spiritual gifts are intended to create a relationship in which I need you and you need me, and we are of one heart, one soul, and one mind. In Jesus' high priestly prayer He prayed:

> **. . . that they all may be one; as thou, Father, art in me, and I in thee, that they also may be one in us: that the world may believe that thou hast sent me (Jn 17:21).**

This is what spiritual gifts are all about. They are for drawing us together to a loving oneness, so that the world may believe that Jesus is indeed the Messiah. The central theme of the whole passage in First Corinthians about Spiritual gifts is this loving oneness. And it is critical because our whole testimony to the world hangs on the loving unity of the body of Christ. Jesus pleaded that the Father would bring about our unity **"that the world may believe that thou hast sent me."** Consider how frequently Paul emphasizes oneness, unity, sameness, as he writes the 12th chapter of First Corinthians:

> **Vs 4: Now there are diversities of gifts, but the same Spirit.**
>
> **Vs 5: And there are differences of administrations, but the same Lord.**
>
> **Vs 6: And there are diversities of operations, but it is the same God which worketh all in all.**
>
> **Vs 7: But the manifestation of the Spirit is given to every man to profit withal."**
>
> **Vs 8: For to one is given by the Spirit the word of wisdom; to another the word of knowledge by the same Spirit;**
>
> **Vs 9: . . . to another faith by the same Spirit; to another the gifts of healing by the same Spirit;**
>
> **Vs 10-11 . . . working of miracles . . . prophecy . . . discerning of spirits . . . tongues . . . interpretation of tongues: but all these worketh that one and the selfsame Spirit . . . .**
>
> **Vs 12: For as the body is one, and hath many members, and all the members of that one body, being many, are one body: so also is Christ.**
>
> **Vs 13: For by one Spirit are we all baptized into one Body . . . and have been all made to drink into one Spirit.**

Paul goes on talking about the necessity of each part of the body with its individual function:

> **Vs 21: And the eye cannot say unto the hand, I have no need of thee: nor again the head to the feet, I have no need of you.**
>
> **Vs 24-26: . . . but God hath tempered the body together, having given more abundant honour to that part**

which lacked: that there should be no schism in the body; but that the members should have the same care one for another. And whether one member suffer, all the members suffer with it; or one member be honoured, all the members rejoice with it.

Enough said? Gifts are about unity, oneness, sameness, a single body **"tempered"** together, **"that there should be no schism in the body."** And the very thing that God chose to use to temper the body together, is nothing other than spiritual gifts. The gifts are the glue that hold the body of Christ together. Therefore, musician, the reason God gave you the gift of instrument playing and/or singing, is none other than to draw the body of Christ together to a loving oneness. Understand this. God did not give you musical gifts simply for your own enjoyment, although there is nothing wrong with enjoying it while you play and sing. He did not give you that gift just so you could make a lot of money, although it is not necessarily wrong to make money while exercising your gift. And He did not give you that gift so you could show off and pridefully flash your gift around to impress people, as if your gift were a diamond ring. Be careful. There is great temptation before all gifted musicians to misuse their gifts. Be careful that accolades and money do not become your primary motivation. God's primary purpose in granting you that gift, that grace, that measure of His own God-like qualities and abilities, is to use it to do your part in drawing the body of Christ together to an interdependent, loving oneness that displays God's character and nature to the world, so the world may believe that Jesus is the Messiah. Exercise your gift with this in mind.

18

GIFTS PRODUCE ONENESS

Suppose you had some terrible, life-threatening sickness, and someone with the gift of healing came along and laid hands on you, prayed, and you were healed. How would you feel toward that person? Or suppose you had a crucial decision to make that you had been wrestling over for weeks, and someone with the gift of the word of wisdom came along and shared with you a word of wisdom from the Lord which was just what you needed to hear to enable you to make the right decision. How would you feel toward that person? Suppose you had been troubled by some great theological question for a long time, and you heard a gifted teacher clearly address the issue and put everything into perspective, he answered all your questions and gave you understanding. How would you feel toward that person?

In all these situations, likely, you would feel indebted to the person who exercised their spiritual gift on your behalf. Because they met the need of the hour for you, a bond would be created, a drawing together would happen. You would probably feel love toward that person, and it would become your heart's desire to return the favor if you could. And you would take delight in spending time with that person, just to be in his presence. So it is with the gifts of the Spirit. Whenever one Christian exercises his gifts on the behalf of another it creates a bond of loving oneness, a unity, an endearment, a mutual dependence, and a desire to be in the presence of one another. We find this occurring throughout the Bible whenever God's people ministered to one another. Perhaps the grandest expression of this phenomenon is in the Book of Acts when spiritual gifts were first imparted to the apostles. First, the gift of tongues was given. Then Peter exercises the gift of teaching and/or preaching, and 3000 souls joined themselves to the church. And look at the results:

> **And all that believed were together, and had all things**
> **common . . . and they, continuing daily with one accord in**
> **the temple, and breaking bread from house to house, did eat**
> **their meat with gladness and singleness of heart (Acts 2:44-46).**

Note the unifying effects of the exercise of these gifts: the believers were together, had all things common, they were of one accord, shared their meals together, and had singleness of heart. Three chapters later we read of gifts of miracles being exercised, with similar results:

> **And by the hands of the apostles were many signs and**
> **wonders wrought among the people; (and they were all with**
> **one accord in Solomon's porch . . . And believers were the**

> **more added to the Lord, multitudes both of men and
> women) (Acts 5:12-14).**

Again, this time by means of the gift of miracles, we have the effect of one accord, and multitudes joining themselves to the church. That is what spiritual gifts are all about, creating oneness, unity, drawing believers together, as Paul explained:

> **But the manifestation of the Spirit is given to every man to
> profit withal (1 Cor 12:7).**

And remember that **"profit withal"** is translated from the Greek, *"sumpheron,"* which literally means, *"to bring together."*

In Bible days spiritual gifts drew believers together, and they still do today. And it is not just preaching, teaching, tongues and miracles that draw Christians together, but the exercise of every gift can do this, including musical gifts. Many times we as a family have experienced this. Wherever we go with our harps, as soon as our children start playing, people are drawn to us and an immediate bond is created as people are blessed and edified by the music. People feel at home with us, of one heart and one accord. We are endeared to one another, just by the exercise of my children's gifts of music. And these are often people that we would have never had any interaction with. But as a result of the exercise of the gift of music, we become instant friends. Though we may have all sorts of differences in Christian doctrine and practice, yet, we find ourselves of one accord, with a kindred spirit, experiencing Christian love toward one another. The unity created is to such a degree that we are frequently invited to present harp programs at churches far different from ours, and their pulpits are open to me.

You know, if ever the church (the world-wide church) was in need of unity, it is in this day and age in which we live. For centuries the church has been dividing, splitting, and splintering over a multitude of issues, such that many Christians today have given up on organized church and have resorted to home-churching. With all the denominational barriers and the disagreements in doctrine and practice, the church today is anything but one. But consider Jesus' prayer for His church;

> **That they all may be one; as thou, Father, art in me, and I in
> thee, that they also may be one in us: that the world may
> believe that thou hast sent me (Jn 17:21).**

True, there are lines to be drawn, especially when organizations cease to be the true church of Jesus Christ. But perhaps we're a bit too quick to draw lines over lesser issues. God's heart for His church is oneness, even as the Father and Son are one. That's a tall order, but not impossible. He gave gifts for this purpose. So be encouraged, musician, for you have a gift that has remarkable ability to produce oneness in the body of Christ, which is at the center of God's heart.

19

THE VARIETY OF THE GIFTS

It is said that no two snow flakes are exactly alike. God has the amazing ability to create things that are the same, yet different. When He made bugs He didn't just make one kind, but thousands of varieties of them. We find the same with birds, fish, plants, animals, microbes, stars, etc. Our God is a God of variety and we find tremendous variation in all of His creation. And when it comes to granting gifts of grace to the members of the body of Christ, God holds true to form:

> **Now there are diversities of gifts, but the same Spirit. And there are differences of administrations, but the same Lord (1 Cor 12:4-5).**

Both words, **"diversities"** and **"differences,"** are translated here from the same Greek word, *"diairesis,"* which, as we have mentioned previously, literally means *"to take apart."* Once again we have the picture of God taking apart or separating the qualities and abilities that Jesus possesses, and distributing them to the individuals in the church. And one group of Jesus' qualities and abilities mentioned here is **"administrations."**

When we use the word *"administration"* today we generally think of someone occupying a position of "authority" who rules in some capacity. But the meaning of that word is very different here. **"Administrations"** is translated from the Greek, *"diakonion,"* which means *"to render any kind of service" (Vine 563).* Our English word for the church office of *"deacon"* is just a transliteration from the Greek, *"diakonos,"* which simply means *"servant" (Vine 147).* If we look closely at the English word, *"administrations,"* we can see the same thought, as the word itself contains the word *"minister,"* which means *"to serve."* So when the Bible speaks of **"differences of administrations"** it is referring to a variety of *"services"* (any services) that God equips and moves anyone to perform for the good of His church. Applications here are quite broad. The first *"deacons"* in the Bible were appointed in the Book of Acts as table waiters, making sure the widows received their portion of food. Needs vary widely today, therefore, services vary widely. A *"service"* can be anything from helping a family move to a new house, to playing an instrument. But the important thing to keep in mind is that the ability to meet various needs is given by **"...the same God which worketh all in all (1 Cor 12:6).** And His purpose is **"to profit withal,"** to draw the body of Christ together to a loving onenesss. The **"differences of administrations"** are simply graces, God-like qualities and abilities that Jesus had. He says of Himself:

> **. . . the Son of man came not to be ministered unto, but to minister, and to give his life a ransom for many (Matt 20:28).**

Of course, His greatest ministry (or service) to mankind was the giving of His life as a ransom, a payment for our sins. But Jesus ministered in many other different ways: healing, teaching, feeding the hungry, changing water to wine, sharing words of wisdom, words of knowledge, prophesying, discerning spirits, helping people...in short, He **"went about doing good (Acts 10:38)."** Indeed, Jesus performed far more services than are recorded in the Bible. John tells us:

> **And there are also many other things which Jesus did, the**
> **which, if they should be written every one, I suppose that**
> **even the world itself could not contain the books that should**
> **be written. Amen (Jn 21:25).**

So this **"differences of administrations"** is quite broad. And to expand it even more, Paul further explains:

> **And there are diversities of operations, but it is the same**
> **God which worketh all in all (1 Cor 12:6).**

The word **"operations"** here is translated from the Greek *"energamaton,"* which means *"workings" (Vine 685).* Our English word "energy" (the ability to perform work) is transliterated from this word *"energamaton."* So once again, **"diversities of operations"** gives us a broad range of "works" referring to any good work we might do in serving, ministering, meeting needs, etc. It is no stretch to say that playing and singing sacred music are included among the **"diversities of operations . . . administrations . . . gifts"** that God, the Holy Spirit, endows on Christians for creating loving unity in the body of Christ. As a musician, you have the opportunity to minister **"grace"** to your listeners. Playing and singing sacred music promotes God-like qualities in your hearers. It brings forth the fruit of the Spirit in them: **"love, joy, peace, gentleness, goodness, faith, meekness,"** all that beautiful fruit of the Spirit just wells up in people when they listen to sacred music. We have seen it many times. I love to watch the audience when my daughters play harps at programs. All over their faces, people just light up with love, joy, faith, peace, etc. They radiate the presence of the Holy Spirit. And you know, there aren't many things in this world that can do that. You have a uniquely powerful instrument in your hands and in your voice, an instrument that can actually change the spirit of a person, or a whole group of people, just by playing and singing a sacred song. If that's not a gift of the Holy Spirit of God, I don't know what is. The most dramatic example of this change, of course, is when David played for Saul. Saul's spirit changed from an angry, murderous rage, to peace, gentleness, and wellness. Just by playing a song David brought Saul from the works of the flesh to the fruit of the Spirit. Just think, at your fingertips (literally) you have this power, just by exercising your gift of music. Hear Paul's exhortation:

> **Even so ye, forasmuch as ye are zealous of spiritual gifts,**
> **seek that ye may excel to the edifying of the church (1 Cor**
> **14:12).**

The word **"edifying"** here is translated from the Greek, *"oikodoman."* This is a two part word. The root word, *"oikos"* means *"a home."* The suffix, *"demo"* means *"to build" (Vine 194).* Just as a carpenter uses his tools and equipment to build a house, so the Christian is to use the spiritual gifts (or graces) given him to build the church, the body of Christ. What could be more **"edifying"** than bringing forth the fruit of the Spirit in God's people? This is what to strive for in your music.

20

HOW TO KNOW WHAT GIFT(S) YOU HAVE

The tag on a typical Christmas gift might read: "To Sally, with love, from Mom and Dad." Though there may be a pile of gifts waiting for any number of different people, everybody can easily tell who gets which gifts, just by the tags. But it's not that way with spiritual gifts. There are no tags, and the Bible does not specifically tell us how to know which gifts we have. The Bible records a few people that God spoke to directly and informed them about their specific gifts and mission in life, but He does not do that with most of us. So how can we find out what gifts we have? Well, since I cannot quote any Bible verse to answer this question, I will share my opinion, and you can take it for what it's worth to you.

In general, I do not believe we have to sit down and try to figure out which gifts we have. It has been my observation that when someone has a gift, he will simply find himself doing it. Most of the time he will enjoy doing it, and he will have this inner compulsion to do this thing. Indeed, he can hardly hold himself back from doing it, because God has put it within him. He will not have to push himself into any position to be able to exercise his gift. Often, others will see the gift in him and ask him to exercise his gift.

Perhaps you have already experienced this with your music. You had this desire to play or sing, this inner compulsion, and you don't know where it came from. You did not manufacture that desire, it was just in you, and you could hardly hold yourself back. And you no sooner got your hands on your instrument, or started to sing, than you found that you were able to, and you were blessed to play and sing. Others recognized that you had a special grace from God to be able to make music, and they asked you to play and sing more. Perhaps they even stood in awe as you played and sang. Your music inspired them to worship, and they praised God because of your musical ability. You may have even felt a sweet endearment between you and your audience, which came about for no other reason than the fact that your music ministered to their souls. Guess what? You have the gift of music.

Now just because someone has a gift, that does not mean he will perform it perfectly from the start, nor does it mean he will never need any practice. He will likely be able to learn it relatively fast, and it may come fairly easy for him, compared to others who may not have the same gift. But there is learning and practicing involved in the exercise of most gifts. A gifted teacher must learn some things about teaching, and he will often learn by making mistakes, but if he is gifted, he will probably catch on fairly quickly. Likewise a gifted musician has some things to learn about making music, and though it may come easily for him, he still must practice to develop his skill. So don't think that you don't have the gift of music just because you make mistakes or need to learn and practice--that's part of being human. Therefore, enjoy and exercise your gift of music, but keep learning, training, and practicing to develop your skill, that you might fulfill the exhortation:

> **Praise the Lord with harp...sing unto him a new song: play skillfully with a loud noise (Ps 33:2-3).**

Paul exhorts along similar lines:

> **. . . Take heed to the ministry which thou hast received in the Lord, that thou fulfill it (Col 4:17).**

21

GOD'S PERSONAL ATTENTION IN GIVING GIFTS

Of the estimated six billion people to whom God has given life on this planet, it is a wondrous thing that no two are exactly alike. God gave each individual his own unique combination of characteristics and abilities, making him distinctly different from all others. Those characteristics and abilities were planned by God before we were born. They begin developing from the moment of conception, and continue to develop throughout life. David marvels at the intimate working of God in fashioning him from the womb:

> **O Lord, thou hast searched me, and known me. Thou knowest my downsitting and mine uprising, thou understandest my thought afar off. Thou compassest my path and my lying down, and art acquainted with all my ways . . . Such knowledge is too wonderful for me; it is high, I cannot attain unto it . . . For thou hast possessed my reins; thou hast covered me in my mother's womb. I will praise thee; for I am fearfully and wonderfully made: marvellous are thy works; and that my soul knoweth full well. My substance was not hid from thee, when I was made in secret, and curiously wrought in the lowest parts of the earth. Thine eyes did see my substance, yet being unperfect; and in thy book all my members were written, which in continuance were fashioned, when as yet there was none of them. How precious also are thy thoughts unto me, O God! How great is the sum of them (Ps 139)!**

How wondrous that God gives such personal attention to the formation of each one of us from the womb! It seems that He labors over every one of us, one at a time, in putting us together. And He is continually fashioning us, individually, into the one-of-a-kind person He has sovereignly ordained us to become. The characteristics, desires, gifts, and abilities each of us has were not only put within us by God, but he planned it so before our conception. God revealed to Jeremiah:

> **Before I formed thee in the belly I knew thee; and before thou camest forth out of the womb I sanctified thee, and I ordained thee a prophet unto the nations (Jer 1:5).**

Long before his birth God had already decided to put the gift of prophecy within Jeremiah. And not only was the gift ordained to be in him, but the desire--indeed, the inner compulsion to prophecy was within Jeremiah, such that he could not restrain himself from prophesying. At one point, after his words were much rejected, Jeremiah reveals:

> **Then I said, I will not make mention of him, nor speak any more in his name. But his word was in mine heart as a burning fire shut up in my bones, and I was weary with forbearing, and I could not stay (Jer 20:9).**

Both the gift and the compulsion to exercise the gift were preplanned and built into Jeremiah's being by God before he was conceived. We find the same with the Apostle Paul, who testifies:

> **But when it pleased God, who separated me from my mother's womb, and called me by his grace, to reveal his Son in me, that I might preach him among the heathen . . . . (Gal 1:15-16).**

Paul's gift of preaching was preplanned and built into Paul's being by God before he was conceived. Paul was separated from the womb for this purpose. And God created a desire (compulsion) to preach so strong within Paul that he says " **. . . woe is unto me, if I preach not the gospel**" (1 Cor 9:16)!

I'd like to suggest that David, Jeremiah and Paul are not special cases, but God labors over each of us the same way. Every one of us is **"fearfully and wonderfully made . . . curiously wrought in the lowest parts of the earth."** Both you and I must say with David:

> **Thine eyes did see my substance, yet being unperfect; and in thy book all my members were written, which in continuance were fashioned, when as yet there was none of them. How precious also are thy thoughts unto me, O God! How great is the sum of them (Ps 139)!**

We serve a big God, don't we? So big that He gives individual, personal attention to the formation of each one of us and preplans our characteristics, abilities, gifts, and even the desire (or compulsion) to exercise those gifts. Know this, O musician, that your musical ability was ordained by God before you were conceived. Even your desire (or compulsion) to make music was preplanned by our Creator. There is only one right response to such knowledge. David put it quite simply:

> **I will praise thee; for I am fearfully and wonderfully made: marvellous are thy works; and that my soul knoweth full well (Ps 139:14).**

22

God's Sovereign Choice in Giving Gifts

As a boy I recall writing a "wish list" every Christmas and birthday. Gifts were coming my way and I wanted to be sure everybody knew what to get me. When the long-anticipated gift-opening moment finally came I ripped each package open with quivering fingers and bulging eyes. Is it? Could it be?--Oh what a let-down!—socks—handkerchiefs—a new shirt. Most disappointing. The only gift that came from my wish list was a Slinky. I didn't get any of the other things I had asked for, not even the motorcycle or the snowmobile. I hadn't even bothered to ask for the set of drums, because, for the most part, my parents made the decisions about which gifts I would have, and which gifts I would not have. And looking back, it's a good thing. My choices probably would have spoiled me, killed me, or driven everybody else in the house crazy. As much as my parents would have liked to have given me everything I desired, they knew what was best for me and for the family. Children just don't always have the wisdom to know what they should ask for. It's the same with my own children. I once asked my six-year old son what he would ask for if he could have anything he wanted in the whole world. Without hesitation he replied, "A yo-yo." And he couldn't understand why I laughed.

Well, I said all that just to say this; Christians, the Church, and the world, are most fortunate that God is the one who decides which spiritual gifts a person receives, and which ones he does not receive. After listing numerous gifts, the Apostle Paul points out:

> **But all these worketh that one and the selfsame Spirit,**
> **dividing to every man severally as he will (1 Cor 12:11).**

Note that it says **"as he will,"** not, as **"we"** will. Paul emphasizes God's sovereign choice further:

> **But now hath God set the members every one of them in the**
> **body, as it hath pleased him (1 Cor 12:18).**

Again, it is **"as it hath pleased Him,"** not, as it hath pleased **"us."**

But every Christian does receive gifts. Some have the mistaken idea that they don't have any gifts and therefore can't do anything in God's kingdom. Paul explains:

> **But the manifestation of the Spirit is given to every man to**
> **profit withal (1 Cor 12:7).**

So **"every man,"** (every individual) is given some manifestation of the Spirit, some grace, some God-like quality or ability with which he can help draw the body of Christ together. You may not be given the same gift your neighbor has, and you may not be given the gift that you would like to have, but every Christian is given some **"manifestation of the Spirit."** The word **"manifestation"** is an interesting word. It is translated from the Greek, *"phanerosis,"* a derivation of *"phaneros,"* meaning *"'open to sight, visible, manifest'(the root phan--, signifying 'shining'. . . .)" (Vine 390).* Isn't that beautiful? It is the gifts that make the Holy Spirit of God open to sight through us. God intends that every one of us make Him visible, shining for all to see. Perhaps you are familiar with the song, "Shine Jesus Shine." It is you and I that make Him shine by exercising our gifts. We might say that you and I actually put God on display on the earth. That is quite a responsibility. While Jesus was on earth He did that perfectly all the time. That's why when one of the disciples asked Him, **". . . Lord, shew us the Father . . . ." (Jn 14:8)** Jesus could say, **" . . . he that hath seen me hath seen the Father . . . ." (Jn 14:9).** For 33 years Jesus put God on display to the world, so that if anybody wanted to know what God looked like, they simply had to observe Jesus. But when He finished His work He ascended into heaven, and with Him went the **"express image of the Father,"** as well as the **"fullness of the Godhead."** He left nothing behind to take His place, except you and me. But He did not abandon us. He sent the Holy Spirit of God to indwell and empower us to put God on display as He did. He did not, however, put **"all the fullness of the Godhead"** into any one individual, but spread it out and gave a little bit of the Godhead to each and every one of us so that each member could put some of the Godhead on display as we exercise our gifts, our graces, our God-like qualities and abilities.

Did you ever think about music making in this respect? You may not be a gifted preacher, or have the gift of working miracles, or have the gift of prophecy, but if your gift is to sing or play sacred music on an instrument, you can make **"manifest"** the Holy Spirit of God. Your song makes Him visible, it makes Him shine, it puts God on display for all the world to see. By His sovereign choice, it pleased God to grant you this gift, that by singing and playing sacred music you would have a part in bonding His people together.

23

STIRRING UP THE GIFTS

Most of us enjoy sitting around a blazing campfire, basking in its radiant warmth and golden glow. But inevitably, after a while the fire begins to die down. We move closer as the light fades and the heat diminishes, but soon we realize something needs to be done. More wood isn't always the answer. Often there is plenty of wood in the fire, but it just isn't burning to its fullest potential. All it needs is a little stirring to restore the lively intensity we enjoyed earlier. Someone has only to get a stick and poke around a bit, stir it up, and we have a nice, revived campfire once again. It's sort of that way with spiritual gifts. Paul exhorts Timothy:

Neglect not the gift that is in thee . . . . (1 Tim 4:14).

The word **"neglect"** here is translated from the Greek, *"ameleo,"* meaning, *"to be careless, not to care," (Vine 429).* In this epistle Paul is telling Timothy to care, care enough about others that he exercise his gift, because others need it. Some time later Paul wrote another epistle to Timothy, and this time Paul reminds Timothy of his **"unfeigned (without hypocrisy) faith,"** that first dwelt in his grandmother, then in his mother, and now in him. This reminder is intended to cause Timothy *"to care,"* and Paul concludes:

**Wherefore I put thee in remembrance that thou stir up the
gift of God which is in thee . . . . (2 Tim 1:6).**

The expression **"stir up"** here is translated from the Greek, *"anazopureo,"* which is a three part word. The prefix, *"ana,"* means *"up, or again."* The middle part, *"zo,"* means *"alive,"* and the root word, *"pureo,"* means, *"fire." (Vine 600).* Literally, **"stir up"** means to *"liven up the fire."* Just like a campfire, **"the gift of God"** can indeed begin to die down through neglect (not caring). Someone needs to get a stick to stir it up, to poke around a bit to restore the warmth and light of the blaze. This is where sacred music comes in for those endowed with the gift of music. How many times have you heard a song referred to as a "stirring song?" It has powerful lyrics, bolstered by an appropriate musical arrangement. These songs cause us *"to care."* They just make you want to get out there and do all you can for God, because you care. And you can sing and play such a song to stir up your own gifts, and to stir up the gifts in others. Consider this one by Frances Havergal:

**Take my life, and let it be
Consecrated, Lord, to Thee;
Take my hands, and let them move**

> **At the impulse of Thy love,**
> **At the impulse of Thy love.**

Lyrics like this, when played and sung, can stir up gifts of mercy, administrations (services), operations (works). These words make us care, care enough to do whatever we can for the Kingdom of the One who loves us. The song continues:

> **Take my feet, and let them be**
> **Swift and beautiful for Thee;**
> **. . .Take my lips, and let them be**
> **Filled with messages from Thee;**

This part can stir up gifts of preaching, teaching, and evangelism.
And to stir up the gift of giving:

> **Take my silver and my gold,**
> **Not a mite would I withhold.**

Here is another well known hymn by Samuel Stone that can stir up gifts. This song first reminds us of our privileged relationship with our Lord, which should cause us to care enough to be willing to exercise our gifts. It then beautifully describes the bond of loving oneness that the gifts are intended to produce:

> **The Church's one Foundation is Jesus Christ her Lord;**
> **She is His new creation by water and the Word:**
> **From heav'n He came and sought her to be His holy Bride;**
> **With His own blood He bought her, and for her life He died.**
>
> **Elect from every nation, yet one o'er all the earth,**
> **Her charter of salvation one Lord, one faith, one birth:**
> **One holy name she blesses, partakes one holy food,**
> **And to one hope she presses, with every grace endued.**

This song, in the last phrase, even mentions the very gifts (graces) with which God has endowed the individuals in the church. Sing and play such songs and you will do much to cause God's people *"to care"* enough to exercise their gifts, and to stir up the gifts (graces) with which we are endued.

24

COMPOUNDING THE GIFTS WITH MUSIC

One of the special blessings of being a gifted musician is the unique opportunity you have to exercise other gifts that you may not have. That sounds like a paradox, I know, but consider the gift-compounding effects of being a gifted musician. You may not have the gift of exhortation, which Paul mentions among the gifts of Romans 12. But as a musician, you can sing and play a song of exhortation and therefore exhort, just like someone who does have that gift. Exhortation is translated from the Greek, *"paraklesis,"* which literally means *"a calling to one's side" (Vine 217).* It gives the picture of walking along, side by side with a brother or sister, arm over their shoulder, and giving an appeal, entreaty, or some words of encouragement. When you're around someone with the gift of exhortation you just feel lifted up and encouraged to press on in the battle. And you can do that with music. Many songs are songs of exhortation, like this one by William Merril:

> **Rise up, O men of God!**
> **Have done with lesser things;**
> **Give heart and soul and mind and strength**
> **To serve the King of kings.**

Don't you feel just lifted up, strengthened, encouraged, motivated, when you hear a song like that? You can exhort with your music.

In First Corinthians 12 Paul mentions a gift which he calls **"the word of wisdom."** He does not define it, and the Greek doesn't help us here, but I'll share my view and you can take it for what it's worth. It seems to me that the gift of **"the word of wisdom"** would be a special ability that God gives to someone to give wise counsel, particularly at a moment when it is most needed. Someone may be wrestling over a decision. He doesn't know which way to turn. Then a brother or sister comes along and shares just the right course of action at just the right time. Perhaps someone needs to take a step of faith, but he just isn't sure, and some musician comes along and shares this song by John Sammis:

> **Trust and obey, for there's no other way**
> **To be happy in Jesus, but to trust and obey.**
> **But we never can prove the delights of His love**
> **Until all on the altar we lay;**
> **For the favor He shows, and the joy He bestows,**
> **Are for them who will trust and obey.**

That is wisdom, and many songs hold such wisdom. You may not have the gift, per-se, but you can give a word of wisdom with your music to someone who is not sure which way to go, or wrestling over some step of faith. And you may not even know that you are ministering to their need at the time.

The gift of evangelism is not specifically named in the Bible, though it certainly would be included in the general gifts of administrations, operations, ministries, and services. It is self-evident that God grants to certain individuals, such as Billy Graham, this gift. It is a special ability to know just what to say, and just how to say it, to win many souls to the Lord. You may not have the gift of evangelism, but you can still evangelize, just by playing and singing an evangelistic song. Here's one by Will Thompson:

> **Softly and tenderly Jesus is calling,**
> **Calling for you and for me;**
> **See, on the portals He's watching and waiting,**
> **Watching for you and for me.**
> **Come home, come home,**
> **Ye who are weary come home!**
> **Earnestly, tenderly, Jesus is calling,**
> **Calling, O sinner, come home!**

You just might bring a sinner to tears of conviction of sin by sharing this evangelistic song, and other songs like it.

Another gift mentioned in First Corinthians 12 is the gift of **"faith"**—the assurance and courage to believe and obey God, even under the most doubt-evoking circumstances. A great portion of all the Christian songs ever written are faith-building songs. You may not have the special gift of faith, but you can build your own faith, as well as the faith of others by playing and singing songs of faith, like this stirring hymn by Charles Wesley:

> **Arise, my soul, arise, shake off thy guilty fears;**
> **A bleeding sacrifice in my behalf appears;**
> **Before the throne my surety stands,**
> **My name is written on His hands.**
>
> **He ever lives above, for me to intercede;**
> **His all-redeeming love, His precious blood to plead;**
> **His blood atoned for all our race,**
> **And sprinkles now the throne of grace.**
>
> **Five bleeding wounds He bears, received on Calvary;**
> **They pour effectual prayers, they strongly speak for me;**

Oh, him forgive! Forgive, they cry,
Nor let the ransomed sinner die.

My God is reconciled, His pard'ning voice I hear;
He owns me for His child, I can no longer fear;
With confidence I now draw nigh,
And Father, Abba, Father, cry. Amen.

That's a real faith-builder. Perhaps you have noticed that some of the other songs we've mentioned also build faith, while they exhort, while they give wisdom, while they evangelize. What a splendid thing music is, that a host of gifts--graces--manifestations of the Holy Spirit, can be exercised and compounded, just by a song. Music is a powerful thing, and you have it, literally, right at your fingertips. With it you can accomplish much in the Kingdom of God: **"I beseech you, therefore, brethren, by the mercies of God, that ye present your bodies a living sacrifice, holy, acceptable unto God, which is your reasonable service" (Rom 12:1).**

25

TO PROPHESY WITH MUSIC

In the Old Testament God spoke to His people through prophets. Prophets were people who received direct revelation from God, and then communicated that revelation to the people. Some of the prophets used musical instruments as an aid in the communication. For example:

> **Moreover David and the captains of the host separated to
> the service of the sons of Asaph, and of Heman, and of
> Jeduthun, who should prophesy with harps, with psalteries,
> and with cymbals: (1 Chron 25:1).**

It goes on to list a little more specifically the types of prophecy the instruments were used for, like the six sons of Jeduthun **"who prophesied with a harp, to give thanks and to praise the Lord"** (1 Chron 25:3).

Then we have Heman's family:

> **All these were the sons of Heman the king's seer in the
> words of God, to lift up the horn. And God gave to Heman
> fourteen sons and three daughters. All these were under the
> hands of their father for song in the house of the Lord, with
> cymbals, psalteries, and harps, for the service of the house of
> God . . . . (1 Chron 25:5-6).**

Lots of others joined them, totaling 288 who were **"instructed in the songs of the Lord, even all that were cunning . . . . "** (1 Chron 25:7). That must have made for quite an ensemble, all prophesying together with instruments. The Bible does not explain exactly how they did the prophesying, but I suppose they took the messages that God gave them and arranged appropriate music that would help to convey the meaning of the words. Perhaps it was sort of like a sermon put to music. Actually, when you think about it, a lot of our hymns are sermons put to music. In fact, many of our hymns are based on prophecy taken straight from the Bible. I don't think I'm stretching things too far to say that if you sing and play such a hymn, you are, in a sense, prophesying with instruments, much as did the Old Testament prophets. Take a hymn like, "Man of Sorrows," one of my favorite hymns. For most of this song Philip Bliss simply followed the prophecy from Isaiah 53 about the suffering Messiah. With slight rewording he arranged some very appropriate music that beautifully expresses the message of the prophecy. Consider the words:

"Man of Sorrows," what a name
For the Son of God who came
Ruined sinners to reclaim!
Hallelujah! What a Savior!

Bearing shame and scoffing rude,
In my place condemned He stood;
Sealed my pardon with His blood;
Hallelujah! What a Savior!

Guilty, vile and helpless, we;
Spotless Lamb of God was He;
"Full atonement!" Can it be?
Hallelujah! What a Savior!

Lifted up was He to die,
"It is finished," was His cry;
Now in heav'n exalted high;
Hallelujah! What a Savior!

When He comes, our glorious King,
All His ransomed home to bring,
Then anew this song we'll sing;
Hallelujah! What a Savior!

That whole song is merely prophecy put to music. Sing it and play it on your instrument, and you are like unto one of God's prophets. This is not to say that simply singing and playing a song containing prophecy makes you a prophet, or endows you with the gift of prophecy. But we can say that you are at least passing on prophecy from one who had the gift of prophecy. And bear in mind that prophecy, as a New Testament gift, is ranked second only to apostleship. It is one of the **"best gifts"** that the church is exhorted to **"covet earnestly" (1 Cor 12:31).** The reasons given are:

> **. . . he that prophesieth speaketh unto men to edification,**
> **and exhortation, and comfort . . . . " (1 Cor 14:3).**

> **. . . if all prophesy, and there come in one that believeth not,**
> **or one unlearned, he is convinced of all, he is judged of all:**
> **And thus are the secrets of his heart made manifest; and so**
> **falling down on his face he will worship God, and report that**
> **God is in you of a truth" (1 Cor 14:24-25).**

This is no small responsibility, and no small honor to share the work of the prophets of God. Remember these things when you sing and play for people, and particularly when you make arrangements for songs. Strive, seek God for His leading to produce arrangements that accurately and powerfully carry and express the meaning of the words. This will require considerable prayer and meditation on the words of a song as you labor to arrange its music, and every time you play and sing it. Paul's exhortation to all:

Follow after charity, and desire spiritual gifts, but rather that ye may prophesy" (1 Cor 14:1).

26

To Teach with Music

You probably learned your ABC's by singing the alphabet. Many have learned the names of the American states and the bones of the body through songs. Lots of Bible verses are put to music to make them easier to remember. I'm rather embarrassed to admit that the only way I can find certain books of the Bible, like Zephaniah, Haggai, and Amos, is by singing the "Books of the Bible" song to myself while I flip through the pages. And stories are often put to music, like the "Song of Moses," so that they will be remembered and passed on. Music has long been used as a means of teaching, and still is, simply because it is a very effective and enjoyable method of teaching. So it's no wonder that the New Testament commands us to use music to teach:

> **Let the word of Christ dwell in you richly in all wisdom;**
> **teaching and admonishing one another in psalms and hymns**
> **and spiritual songs, singing with grace in your hearts to the**
> **Lord" (Col 3:16).**

Please notice here that the thing that causes the **"word of Christ"** to **"dwell in you richly,"** is **"teaching and admonishing one another in psalms and hymns and spiritual songs."** Music is the means of teaching. And the promised effect is great, that the **"word of Christ"** will **"dwell in you richly."** And bear in mind that the word **"psalms"** is translated from the Greek, *"psalmos,"* which means *" . . . a striking or twitching with the fingers (on musical strings)', then, 'a sacred song, sung to musical accompaniment, a psalm'" (Vines 497).* The *"musical strings"* being referred to here, in all likelihood, are the strings of a harp, or at least a harp-like instrument such as a psaltery or lyre.

As a musician, whether you have the "gift of teaching" or not, you can still "teach" with your music. Many hymns are filled with solid, doctrinal teaching. The hymn writer Fanny Crosby (who wrote over 8000 hymns, and was an accomplished harpist herself) once commented that people learn as much theology from hymns as sermons. It's true. Consider some of the lyrics from George Bernard's, "The Old Rugged Cross:"

> **To the old rugged cross I will ever be true,**
> **Its shame and reproach gladly bear;**

Here we have some sound doctrinal teaching about the reproach of the cross that every Christian must bear if he is going to be a faithful witness for the Lord. The message of the cross reduces proud, self-righteous man to a wretched sinner who deserves only God's wrath. This message is offensive to those who view themselves as righteous and worthy of heaven, who have no need of a Savior to atone for their sin. And the cross calls men to repent of their sin. This also is offensive to those who have fearlessly violated God's commands, thinking that their own, self-determined moral code will justify them in God's sight. Starting with Jesus and the apostles, the message of the cross of Christ has always been so offensive to the unrepentant that persecution and suffering have been the Christian's lot in this life.

> **For the preaching of the cross is to them that perish foolishness . . . . " (1 Cor 1:18).**

> **For therefore we both labour and suffer reproach . . . ." (1 Tim 4:10).**

Persecution and suffering is a truth, a doctrine that is well taught in the Bible, and a musician can teach that doctrine just by singing and playing a song like "The Old Rugged Cross." The song goes on to say:

> **Then He'll call me some day to my home far away, Where His glory forever I'll share.**

Again, more sound teaching, giving consolation to those who have suffered for His name's sake. Look at the contrast. During this life--shame and reproach; during the next life--glory. Isn't that just like God? He knows how to balance the scales:

> **So also is the resurrection of the dead . . . It is sown in dishonour; it is raised in glory . . . . " (1 Cor 15:42-43).**

> **If we suffer, we shall also reign with him (2 Tim 2:11-12).**

You can teach these truths, and countless others, just by singing and playing songs that emphasize the doctrinal truths taught in the Bible. And you may well be able to reach people with your music who would otherwise never be reached. Fanny Crosby said it well:

> **. . . many people will read a song who will not read a sermon (Emurian 103).**

27

ENHANCING OTHER GIFTS WITH MUSIC

In any modern war ground troops are usually not sent on a mission into enemy territory without first barraging the enemy camp with artillery. Big guns are strategically placed in the air, land and sea. They are fired to weaken the enemy's defenses, shake them up, pull down strongholds, destroy fortifications. Then the infantry moves in to take the ground, yet they are still supported by the artillery and can call for extra fire power at any time and at most any place. And the success of the campaign is due to the cooperative efforts of everyone involved doing his part.

In a very real sense, the Christian life is a war. The Bible often uses military terms to describe who we are and what we do.

In evangelism, the battleground is the souls of men, ground held by Satan and his allies (the world and the flesh). The ground troops are the preachers, the ones who march into enemy territory to take ground for God's Kingdom. And the artillery, of all things, is music. Perhaps you never thought of music as a big gun, strategically placed to barrage the enemy camp, weaken defenses, pull down strongholds, and destroy fortifications. Music is the artillery that often paves the way for the ground troops to move in and take the ground. Ira Sankey, who worked closely with D. L. Moody as song leader in the great evangelistic campaigns of the late 19th and early 20th centuries, stated that:

> *the success of the Moody-Sankey evangelistic campaigns was*
> *due, more than any other human factor, to the use of Fanny*
> *Crosby's hymns (Osbeck 236).*

And of Sankey himself:

> *it was frequently said that Sankey was as effective a preacher of*
> *the gospel with his songs as D.L. Moody was with his sermons*
> *(Osbeck 90).*

Consider what goes on at an evangelistic campaign. Certain songs are played or sung as the meeting begins, before any preaching is done. This is not just to kill time as the late arrivals find seats, it is to soften hearts and prepare them to receive the spoken word. Then the message is preached, and even as the preacher draws his message to a close, while he is yet speaking, the music begins. The music supports his message, drives it home--gives it more umph! The preacher concludes with an altar call, and then stops speaking. But the music continues for a second verse, rehearsing the truths the preacher expounded. Then a third verse, a fourth, and maybe a fifth, wooing the sinner to consider his ways, count the cost, reflect on eternity, and weigh his decision to repent, or continue his life of sin under Satan's dominion. And for those who raise the white flag of surrender to the King of kings, mercy is extended. And those recipients of mercy gladly change uniforms, and become members of God's army. Hallelujah!

Can you see the beautiful interplay of spiritual gifts in this battle? Of course, it all begins with prayer warriors who have the gift of faith, praying for a harvest of souls. People with the gift of giving provide the funds for all the financial expenses. More people with the gift of helps organize, publicize, and set up the facility. As the crowd gathers gifted musicians and singers provide the music to prepare hearts for the message. The gifted evangelist speaks. His message is supported, amplified, and enhanced by more music, written by gifted song writers. Seeking souls come forward, prepared to surrender to God, and people with the gift of the word of wisdom provide wise counsel to them, individually, to help them make full confession of sin, find true repentance and forgiveness, and place their trust in the blood of Christ to wash their sins away. Everyone has his part, and all are necessary.

I said all that just to say that musicianship is not only a gift in itself, but it can be used to enhance, or aid, or amplify other gifts. And the gift of evangelism is not the only gift that music enhances. Teaching is commonly enhanced by music. If a pastor gives a Sunday morning teaching sermon on the resurrection of Christ, what sort of songs do you suppose will be chosen?—"Christ the Lord is Risen Today." Suppose a message on revival is preached—you can be sure they'll do songs like "Send the Old Time Power". You can count on it, songs are chosen that support and amplify a message, because the gift of music enhances gifts of teaching, preaching, and evangelism. More than once I have heard a preacher break into a song right in the middle of a sermon because the song could express the truth he was trying to share better than any words he could speak.

In a previous section we noted that at least some of the Old Testament prophets prophesied with harps. Why? Because the harp was the instrument of choice to provide the music that would enhance the gift of prophecy. In more recent times the instrument of choice has been the organ and/or piano, and of late, worship bands have become quite popular. Our family does a lot of programs in which I preach a message, but the message is greatly enhanced by my children's harp playing. We use some other instruments as well, but the harp is the central feature. The music itself has a message, and it supports and enhances my message. My children's music makes my message sound substantially better than it would sound alone. Without the support of my family's music, I'm really not much of a speaker. We get lots of requests for family programs, but it's pretty rare that I'm asked to speak alone. I rest in Paul's encouraging words, **". . . but God hath tempered the body together, having given more abundant honour to that part which lacked" (1 Cor 12:24).**

But for you, as a gifted musician, you not only have the ability to minister with your own gifts, but you can even enhance the gifts of others. Remember, therefore, God's purpose in giving spiritual gifts, and His exhortation to us all:

> **Endeavouring to keep the unity of the Spirit in the bond of peace. There is one body, and one Spirit, even as ye are called in one hope of your calling . . . But unto every one of us is given grace according to the measure of the gift of Christ . . . And he gave some, apostles; and some, prophets; and some, evangelists; and some, pastors and teachers; For the perfecting of the saints, for the work of the ministry, for the edifying of the body of Christ: Till we all come in the unity of the faith, and of the knowledge of the Son of God, unto a perfect man, unto the measure of the stature of the fulness of Christ (Eph 4:3-13).**

PART 6

Godly Music

"SO THE KING AND ALL THE CHILDREN OF ISRAEL
DEDICATED THE HOUSE OF THE LORD"
(1 KINGS 8:63).

28

Discernment in Music

Thus far in this devotional guide we have given considerable attention to God's appreciation for music. We've noted that He goes so far as to grant spiritual gifts of music to individuals within His church **"to profit withal,"** meaning, to draw us together to a bond of loving oneness. We enjoy music, are blessed and edified by it, and God Himself is blessed by music as well.

These thoughts, however, as precious as they are, raise some very big questions which we will consider in this section of the devotional guide. Questions like: Does God appreciate all forms of music? Might there be some types of music that God does not appreciate? And does all music edify God's church? Could there be some kinds of music that do not edify the church?

We live in a day when it is rather difficult to even define music, let alone discern the good and the bad. In attempting to establish a definition for the word "music," the Microsoft Encarta Encyclopedia states:

> *One of the legacies of 20ᵗʰ century music is to have blurred*
> *the definition of music as never before (Microsoft 1).*

For example, the sound of a metal-stamping machine was copyrighted as a musical composition, performed, and recorded. Likewise was a reading of a list of hundreds of unrelated objects, activities, and states of mind. One so-called "artist" went so far as to perform, record, and copyright 4 minutes and 33 seconds of silence.

Most of us would have little difficulty discerning these extreme, ridiculous products of our contemporary music world, but other, less divergent forms of music raise questions that are not so easy to answer. What about the beat of certain songs, and what about the rhythm? Does God appreciate the use of synthesizers? And what of certain kinds of notes, and the way music affects a person's body? What if it makes you tap your foot? Does God appreciate that? And what about styles of music? Does God like classical music? How about Country Western, Blue Grass, New Age, Jazz, Christian rock, Christian pop, and Christian rap? And what of secular music in all its forms, how does God feel about that? And, dare I ask, what about the very hymns in our hymnals? Does God truly enjoy them? All of them? How do we know? On what basis do we presume that God is truly blessed by our hymns, and that His church is indeed edified by them?

In attempting to answer these questions various speakers and writers today take some very opposing sides, and usually have some fairly convincing arguments on both sides. Often, what one man approves, another condemns, leaving the honest, seeking soul rather confused and disappointed. The problem is that the Bible never directly addresses most of these questions. We are forced to deal with music in the same way we are forced to deal with many issues that the Bible does not address--it's called *discernment*.

Most of us would agree that smoking is wrong, God does not approve. Even though the Bible never once mentions smoking directly, we can *discern* its wrongness, based on everything the Bible does address, like: **"Know ye not that ye are the temple of God, and that the Spirit of God dwelleth in you? If any man defile the temple of God, him shall God destroy; for the temple of God is holy, which temple ye are" (1 Cor 3:16-17).** That eliminates smoking in most of our minds, as it does drugs and abortion, which are never directly mentioned in the Bible either. So when it comes to music, our only option is to prayerfully consider the things that God *has* addressed in the Bible, and then attempt to make proper applications to music. We'll have to try (as much as possible) to put our personal biases aside, and our prejudices, so that our conclusions are based on something more than personal preference. Let's be careful not to fall into the trap of thinking, "if I like it, then it's good and God approves, and if I don't like it, then it's wrong and God does not approve." Personal preference is no basis for determining the rightness or wrongness of something in God's sight. And neither is public approval. Just because a singer or musician becomes popular in our present world, that is not necessarily evidence of God's approval. John Lennon, of the Beatles, publicly proclaimed that he was more popular than Jesus Christ. And perhaps he was, but one would have considerable reason to question Mr. Lennon's popularity with God.

It should be mentioned here that, as much as we all wish that God would have revealed His heart's attitude concerning all these questions about music, it is very good for us to be forced to seek, search, ponder, study, pray, and meditate on such questions. God could have spelled it all out for us in the Bible, but He wants us to learn to discern. It is an important part of our relationship with Him. After all, someday we will reign with Him, the Bible tells us. And in order to reign we will have to be able to make good judgments without having to run to Him over every nit-picky question. Thus He explains:

> **For every one that useth milk is unskillful in the word of righteousness: for he is a babe. But strong meat belongeth to them that are of full age, even those who by reason of use have their senses exercised to discern both good and evil (Heb 5:13-14).**

The word **"discern"** here comes from the Greek, *"diakrisis,"* which means *"a distinguishing, a clear discrimination, discerning, judging (Vine 171).* Discernment is about making judgments, distinguishing, or separating the good from the evil. If there is such a thing as ungodly (evil) music that displeases God and has negative effects on God's people, every one of us ought to be very concerned about making this separation.

29

THE PRINCIPLE OF SEPARATION
(PART 1)

Recently I discovered something new about God that I never noticed before—He does a lot of separating. This principle has great implications for us in all areas of life. From the very beginning and all through history God has been separating, dividing, and setting apart. He continues to separate today, and He will do more in the future. Consider the days of creation, for example:

In the beginning God created the heaven and the earth (Gen 1:1).

Here is the first great separation, the heaven is distinguished from the earth, two separate localities. Then, still on the very first day:

. . . darkness was upon the face of the deep . . . and God said,
Let there be light: and there was light. And God saw the
light, that it was good: and God divided the light from the
darkness (Gen 1:2-4).

A second great divide takes place, light from darkness. Now we have two distinct, separate states of illumination. Then comes the second day:

And God said, Let there be a firmament in the midst of the
waters, and let it divide the waters from the waters. And
God made the firmament, and divided the waters which
were under the firmament from the waters which were
above the firmament . . . . (Gen 1:6-7).

Now we have a subdivision: the water above (heavenly water) is separated from the water below (earthly water). The dividing line is the air, the atmosphere. The subdivisions continue into the third day:

And God said, Let the waters under the heaven be gathered
together unto one place, and let the dry land appear . . . . (Gen 1:9).

So God gathered the earthly water together into seas, thus separating the water from the dry land. Next comes the fourth day:

**And God said, Let there be lights in the firmament of the
heaven to divide the day from the night (Gen 1:14).**

Another great divide takes place, the division of day and night, accomplished by the sun, moon and stars. The fifth day arrives:

**And God said, Let the earth bring forth abundantly the
moving creature that hath life . . . the fowl . . . whales . . . fish
. . . after their kind (Gen 1: 20-21).**

Another great separation comes to pass--the living from the non-living. This time God creates living creatures that have the breath of life in them, distinct from the non-living objects that He previously created. Among the living creatures we have the general subdivision of water dwellers from those that fly in the firmament. And those two categories are separated into thousands of different species, each able to reproduce only after his own kind, with the species barrier being the dividing line so that each species might remain separate, distinct, different from the rest.

Does the symbolism of all of this strike you as it does me? God separates heaven from earth, light from darkness, waters above from waters below, day from night, living from non-living. Could it be that God intended all this separating to be symbolic, types and shadows of the two kingdoms? God's Kingdom, the sphere of all that is good and Godly, is typified by light, life, and the higher location. Satan's kingdom, the realm of evil and that which is Satanic, is typified by darkness, non-life (or death), and the lower location? Bear in mind that, chronologically, these days of creation (and separation) all happened after Lucifer and his demons were separated from God and his angels. The war between the kingdom of darkness and the kingdom of light was already underway. That war continues to this very day and manifests itself in every area of life on this planet, including music. This is why discernment in music is so necessary. Satan has succeeded in blurring the definition of music in our day. He has enticed musicians to blend the music of the two kingdoms. And to make matters worse, he has also deceived our world into thinking that discernment (separating and judging), in itself, is evil, and convinced our society that *tolerance* is the ultimate good. Remember the key verse in our discussion of Godly music:

**For every one that useth milk is unskillful in the word of
righteousness: for he is a babe. But strong meat belongeth to
them that are of full age, even those who by reason of use
have their senses exercised to discern both good and evil
(Heb 5:13-14).**

God does a lot of separating, and He calls us to do the same. As a musician you have a very great challenge on your hands--to discern between the good and the evil in music.

30

THE PRINCIPLE OF SEPARATION
(PART 2)
GOOD FROM EVIL

Ever since evil was first manifest in the universe, God has been separating, dividing, and setting apart the good from the evil. It all began when rebellious Lucifer and his fallen angels were separated from God and His holy angels. That was just the beginning of the separating. When Adam and Eve sinned they were separated from the beautiful Garden of Eden. The serpent who enticed them to sin was separated from all other creatures and cursed above all. Faithful Noah and his family were separated from their ungodly society and were saved, while the rest were destroyed. Abram was told to separate himself from his heathen family and community and go to the Promised Land, a special parcel of ground that was set apart for Abram and his descendants. God's promise to Abram was to make of him a great nation that would be separate from the heathen nations, and once that nation was established God told them:

> **. . . I am the Lord your God, which have separated you from other people . . . And ye shall be holy unto me: for I the Lord am holy, and have severed you from other people, that ye should be mine (Lev 20:24-26).**

One of the primary purposes for which God instituted the Levitical priesthood was to maintain that separation by teaching the people. Here is God's job description for the priests:

> **And they shall teach my people *the difference* between the holy and profane, and cause them to discern between the unclean and the clean (Ez 44:23).**

There were many times when Israel sinned and failed to remain separate. They mingled with the heathen. They learned the ways of the heathen, intermarried with them, and worshipped their idols. Sometimes the Israelites repented and separated themselves again:

> **And the seed of Israel separated themselves from all strangers, and stood and confessed their sins, and the iniquities of their fathers (Neh 9:2).**

So throughout the Old Testament period we find the principle of separation most prominent, and utterly necessary in order for God's people to remain in proper relationship with Him. And when Jesus instituted the New Testament the principle of separation remained unchanged, as Jesus told His disciples:

> **If ye were of the world, the world would love his own; but because ye are not of the world, but I have chosen you out of the world, therefore the world hateth you (Jn 17:16).**

God's New Testament church is commanded:

> **. . . come out from among them, and be ye separate, saith the Lord, and touch not the unclean thing . . . . (2 Cor 6:17).**

In fact, the word **"church"** is actually translated from the Greek, *"ekklesia,"* the prefix, *"ek,"* meaning *"out,"* and the root word, *"klesis,"* meaning *"a calling" (Vine 42).* The church is the gathering of *"called out ones,"* those who have been called out of the evil world in which we live and called into the family of God. Perhaps you have noticed that Christians don't exactly fit in with the world system, or at least we're not supposed to. If we do, something is wrong, because the Bible says:

> **Ye are a chosen generation, a royal priesthood, an holy nation, a peculiar people: that ye should shew forth the praises of him who hath called you out of darkness into his marvelous light . . . I beseech you as strangers and pilgrims, abstain from fleshly lusts . . . . (1 Pet 2:9-11).**

The phrase, **"a peculiar people,"** does not mean "weird" people, it means a people for *"God's own possession" (Vine 477,)* as separate, distinct, set apart from those who are not God's own. So it is for the present church age, and in the future there will be more dividing and separating:

> **And before him shall be gathered all nations: and he shall separate them one from another, as the shepherd divideth his sheep from the goats (Matt 25:46).**

> **So shall it be at the end of the world: the angels shall come forth and sever the wicked from among the just (Matt 24:40).**

This time the separation will be forever so that God's heaven will be pure and undefiled, eternally separated from evil:

**And there shall in no wise enter into it any thing that
defileth, neither whatsoever worketh abomination, or
maketh a lie: but they which are written in the Lamb's book
of life (Rev 21:27).**

Here we find the ultimate purpose of all the separating--a pure heaven. Can you imagine what heaven would be like if evil were not separated out? Why, it would be no different from this present world. When you come right down to it, in one sense, it's all really very simple. Those who love God and His ways are welcome to enjoy eternity with Him, while those who love the world and the ways of the world (sin) will spend eternity with all those of like mind, separated from God and His people. But while we live in this world, which happens to be Satan's domain, we are called to be separate, holy, peculiar, distinct from the rest of the world, in all areas of life. That includes music. But we will not be able to discern between the good and the evil in music unless we have our **"senses exercised to discern both good and evil" (Heb 5:14).**

31

THE SACRED AND THE SECULAR
(PART 1)

In a certain sense, music can be generally separated into two distinct categories, the *"sacred"* and the *"secular."* What do these words mean?

> *sacred – 1 Set apart or dedicated to religious use: hallowed*
> *(Funk & Wagnalls 1150).*

This English word, *"sacred,"* is translated from the Greek: *hieros – denotes "consecrated to God" (Vine 543).* A synonym of *"sacred"* is the word *"holy:"*

> *holy – 1 Pertaining to holiness; morally excellent; of highest*
> *spiritual purity. 2 Set apart for the service of God or for sacred*
> *uses; consecrated; hallowed (Funk & Wagnalls 635).*

This English word, *"holy,"* is translated from the Greek: *hagios – fundamentally signifies "separated". . . consecrated to God, sacred (Vine 307).* Another synonym of *"sacred"* is the word *"hallow,"* which is translated from the Greek: *hagiazo – "to make holy" (from hagios, "holy"), signifies to set apart for God, to sanctify, to make a person or thing the opposite of koinos, "common" (Vine 287).*

Are you getting the picture? Sacred music is music that is set apart and exclusively devoted to honoring, magnifying, promoting, and glorifying God. It is special, not common, and focuses our attention on God and the things of God. It was written to please God and edify His church. Sacred music includes works such as Handel's Messiah, which is pure Scripture put to music. Hymns, old Gospel pearls like "Amazing Grace" and "How Great Thou Art" are sacred music, as are contemporary choruses such as "We Will Glorify the King of Kings" and "These are the Days of Elijah." Some classical composers such as Handel and Bach wrote numerous instrumental pieces, music with no words, that were written and dedicated unto the glory of God. By definition this too is sacred music, as are numerous works of contemporary Christian artists who write and perform God-honoring music. What a joy to sing and play sacred music. It is the expression of the soul that is in right relationship with God, that loves the Lord God with the whole heart, soul, mind and strength. And how blessed we are in this day and age to have such a large body of sacred music to pick from. I believe that if a musician played nothing but sacred music his whole life he could never learn all that is available.

32

THE SACRED AND THE SECULAR
(PART 2)

As a musician you have probably already been asked to sing or play secular songs, and perhaps you have never considered whether or not there is anything wrong with secular music. After all, much of it doesn't seem overtly evil, and if it has a nice tune and nice words--why not? Well, let's try to clarify some of the issues.

> *secular – 1 pertaining to this world or present life; worldly. 2*
> *not sacred; profane (Funk & Wagnalls 1183).*

So secular music, by definition, is of this world, worldly, and has nothing to do with God. Understand what this means. Secular music does not promote or honor God, although it generally promotes and honors something else. Secular music does not magnify and glorify God, though it usually magnifies and glorifies something else. Secular music does not focus our attention on God, though it does focus our attention on something else. Secular music was not written to please God, though it was written to please someone other than God. Secular music does not edify God's church, though it may well have some other effect on God's church.

Anything and everything could be the subject of secular music, only God must not be. I grew up during the 60's when one of the primary themes of music was love and romance, although it was generally the world's twisted view of love and romance. Such songs often talked about winning and losing at love, as if it were a contest, and then getting revenge on the one that did you wrong. Nancy Sinatra did a song called "Boots" about her old boyfriend who wronged her. She sang; "These boots are made for walkin, and that's just what they'll do, one of these days these boots are gonna walk all over you." It was not unlike the multitudes of country western songs about somebody's "cheatin heart" and those who "done somebody wrong."

Secular songs might honor and glorify something in nature, like John Denver's "Rocky Mountain High," or, "Almost Heaven," "West Virginia." Sometimes holidays were sung about, or a country, somebody's homeland, the idea of freedom, or warfare. Bob Dylan, of the 60's, along with numerous other pop singers and groups of the day, glorified rebellion against authority in songs like: "The Times They are A-Changin," singing, " . . . come mothers and fathers throughout the land, and don't criticize what you can't understand, your sons and your daughters are beyond your command . . . ." The music of that day glorified immorality, drugs, alcohol, fast cars, the beach, surfing, etc. Occasionally, some 60's singers actually came out with something fairly profound, or an accurate observation of life and the way people are. In his song called, "The Boxer," Paul Simon sang, ". . . all lies and jest, still a man hears what he wants to hear and disregards the rest." Yet other singers honored and glorified absolute non-sense. They sang a bunch of statements that rhymed and were put to music, but made no sense and had no message, like this one: "Bye Bye Miss American Pie, drove my Chevy to the levy but the levy was dry, them good ol boys was drinkin whisky and rye, singin this'll be the day that I die . . . ." Then there was the music of the 50's, some of which had very little human language. People actually paid money to listen to singers go: "Doo wop Doo wop Doo wop Doo wop. Waa Waa, Waa Waa . . . ." And since those days, in more recent times, much pop music has taken a turn to give honor and glory to blatantly evil things like hatred, murder, suicide, occultism, and Satan himself. So, whatever the subject, by definition, secular music excludes God and gives honor and glory to anything else. Some of those things may be good in themselves, some may be evil, but by definition, secular music must exclude God. This is the nature of secular music. Some secular songs may give God an honorable (or dishonorable) mention, but that does not make the song sacred, since something other than God is still the primary subject of the song. Secular music is about the world and the things of the world, and stands in marked contrast to sacred music, which is all about God and the things of God. So the sacred is separated, set apart, from the secular. This is the first great divide in music.

33

THE CHRISTIAN AND THE NON-CHRISTIAN

Just as music can be divided into two general categories, the sacred and the secular, likewise people can be divided into two categories, the Christian and the non-Christian. Let's bring into focus the distinctions here. The Bible uses the term "Christian" only a couple of times in referring to those who are followers of Christ. Other terms are used more frequently, such as saints, brethren, believers, or the church. In opening his epistles the Apostle Paul often wrote, **"to the saints,"** referring to all the Christians at the church to whom he was writing. The word **"saint"** is translated from the Greek *"hagios,"* which happens to be the same word from which **"holy"** is translated. Recall that **"holy"** means set apart for the service of God or for sacred uses. It means separation or consecration to God, hallowed, not common. That refers to every Christian, according to the Bible. Every member of Christ's church is a saint, a holy one. And bear in mind that the word **"church"** literally means *"called out."* We are called out of the secular world, the world that excludes God. We are called out and set apart, separated, dedicated, consecrated to God, just as sacred music is holy and set apart from secular worldly music. The apostle Paul greets the church in Ephesus this way:

> **Paul, an apostle of Jesus Christ by the will of God, to the
> saints which are at Ephesus, and to the faithful in Christ
> Jesus . . . who hath blessed us with all spiritual blessings in
> heavenly places in Christ; according as he hath chosen us in
> him before the foundation of the world, that we should be
> holy . . . . (Eph 1:1-4).**

Why did God choose us before the foundation of the world? Was it not **"that we should be holy?"** He wants us to be set apart, dedicated to God, just like sacred music is holy, set apart and dedicated to God. Paul continues:

> **. . . that we should be holy and without blame before Him in
> love; having predestinated us unto the adoption of children
> by Jesus Christ to himself, according to the good pleasure of
> his will, to the praise of the glory of his grace (Eph 1:4-6).**

For what purpose has He predestinated us? It was **"to the praise of the glory of his grace."** Just as sacred music is dedicated to the praise of the glory of God's grace, so are we. Five verses later Paul reemphasizes this thought:

> . . . being predestinated according to the purpose of him who
> worketh all things after the counsel of his own will; that we
> should be to the praise of his glory . . . . (Eph 1:11-12).

So a second time Paul rehearses God's purpose in predestinating us, **"that we should be to the praise of his glory."** And just to make sure we don't miss the point, two verses later he repeats it a third time:

> . . . ye were sealed with that holy Spirit of promise . . . unto
> the praise of his glory (Eph 1: 13-14).

Get the picture? His choosing of us, His predestinating of us, His sealing, are all for one purpose, that we should be holy, **"unto the praise of His glory."** To us He gave life:

> And you hath he quickened, who were dead in trespasses
> and sins, wherein in time past ye walked according to the
> course of this world . . . . (Eph 2:1-2).

We walked **"according to the course of this world,"** this secular world that excludes God and does secular music that excludes God, music that is all about the world and the things of the world. We sang the praises of this world, which, in reality, is **"according to the prince of the power of the air, the spirit that now worketh in the children of disobedience"** (Eph 2:2). The **"prince"** being referred to here is none other than Satan himself.

Is it any wonder that secular music excludes God? Satan wants nothing more than for people to exclude God:

> . . . among whom also we all had our conversation in time past
> in the lusts of our flesh, fulfilling the desires of the flesh and of the mind,
> and were by nature the children of wrath, even as others (Eph 2:3).

Paul wants us to remember who we were:

> Wherefore remember, that ye being in time past Gentiles . . .
> ye were without Christ, being aliens from the commonwealth of Israel,
> and strangers from the covenants of promise, having no hope,
> and without God in the world (Eph 2:11-12).

Remember, we were secular, without God in this secular world. And out of that mess that we were part of, God chose us out and called us out and predestinated us to be a group of people for His own possession. His purpose--that we should be holy and set apart from the disobedient, unbelieving world that excludes God, that we should be separated unto the praise of His glory.

With all that said, there is one very important question for every Christian to answer, and particularly every Christian musician—What are we, as Christians, to do with secular music?

34

A CHOICE WORTH CONSIDERING
(PART 1)

There are some Christians and some Christian musicians who have chosen to dedicate themselves to sacred music, and only sacred music. If you haven't guessed already, I am one who has made this choice. Permit me to share the reasoning that brought me to this conclusion, and you may chose as seems best to you.

To begin, suppose Jesus were to visit your home and ask you to play a song for Him. What would you play? Suppose He tagged along with you every place you went with your instrument. What sort of music would you feel comfortable playing in His presence? You know, He really does visit your home, and He really does tag along with you every place you go, for He said:

". . . I am with you always, even unto the end of the world" (Matt 28:20).

What sort of music do you suppose Jesus listened to and sang when He was physically on the earth? And what would be His musical choice if He were physically present today? I find it rather difficult to image Jesus walking around humming, "I wish they all could be California girls." It seems a safe presumption that Jesus would have chosen only sacred music.

Recall that a Christian is one who follows Christ. On our part, we look to His example and seek to emulate Him in every way possible. On God's part:

For it is God which worketh in you both to will and to do of his good pleasure (Phil 2:13).

For whom he did foreknow, he also did predestinate to be conformed to the image of his Son . . . . (Rom 8:29).

You judge. Is it fitting for those who are being conformed to the image of Christ to be involved with secular, worldly music?

Secular music was a big part of my former, secular, sinful life as an unbeliever, but that life ended when I was reborn of God.

> **If any man be in Christ, he is a new creature; old things are
> passed away; behold, all things are become new" (2 Cor. 5:17).**

My old secular life with its secular music is passed away, I'm now a new creature, and God has **"put a new song in my mouth,"** as the psalmist proclaims:

> **He brought me up out of an horrible pit, out of the miry
> clay, and set my feet upon a rock, and established my goings.
> And he hath put a new song in my mouth, even praise unto
> our God. Many shall see it and fear, and shall trust in the
> Lord (Ps 40:2-3).**

After all my God has done for me, there simply is nothing else worth singing about. My new life has a **"new song, even praise unto our God."**

As a Christian I am no longer a secular person with no relationship with God, but I am now a saint:

> **Now therefore ye are no more strangers and foreigners, but
> fellowcitizens with the saints, and of the household of God
> (Eph 2:19).**

Recall that a **"saint"** is a holy one, separated, set apart for God's own possession. How fitting would it be for a *"holy one"* to be involved with unholy music, a *"separated, set-apart one"* to do unseparated, unset-apart music? How fitting would it be for one of *"God's own possession"* to be involved with the music of those who are not God's own possession?

As Christians we are:

> **fellowcitizens with the saints and of the household of God;
> and are built upon the foundation of the apostles and
> prophets, Jesus Christ himself being the chief corner stone;
> In whom all the building fitly framed together groweth unto
> an holy temple in the Lord; In whom ye also are builded
> together for an habitation of God through the spirit (Eph 2:19-22).**

Notice that we are God's **"holy temple,"** God's **"habitation."** He lives in us. Our very bodies are His dwelling place, His house. He takes up residence in our hearts and inhabits our gatherings. What sort of music do you suppose God prefers to have playing in His house? For that matter, what sort of music do you suppose He listens to in heaven? The Bible records a number of songs that are actually sung in heaven. How many of those songs are worldly, secular songs? Consider a few of the exhortations the New Testament gives us contrasting the world and heaven:

> **If ye then be risen with Christ, seek those things which are above, where Christ sitteth on the right hand of God. Set your affection on things above, not on things on the earth. For ye are dead, and your life is hid with Christ in God (Phil 3:1).**

> **. . . the world is crucified unto me, and I unto the world (Gal 6:14).**

> **And be not conformed to this world: but be ye transformed by the renewing of your mind, that ye may prove what is that good, and acceptable, and perfect, will of God (Rom 12:2).**

Having said such things, would God place His stamp of approval on worldly, secular music? He has more to say about this:

> **Love not the world, neither the things that are in the world. If any man love the world, the love of the Father is not in him. For all that is in the world, the lust of the flesh, and the lust of the eyes, and the pride of life, is not of the Father, but is of the world (1 Jn 2:15-16).**

> **. . . know ye not that the friendship of the world is enmity with God? whosoever therefore will be a friend of the world is the enemy of God (James 4:4).**

Strong words, worthy of much meditation. What room is there in the life of a Christian for secular music that is *"worldly"* by definition?

35

A Choice Worth Considering
(Part 2)

Each of our lives proclaims a *life message,* or, what is often called, *"our testimony."* All that we do and don't do, what we say and do not say, what we wear, where we go, how we interact with others--all of it declares who we are, what values we hold, what God we serve. And if there is one dead give-away as to what we are all about, it is the music we listen to, sing, and play. What message is a Christian sending to the unbelieving world around him when he is involved in worldly, secular music? Jesus spoke plainly and forcefully about this:

> **Ye are the salt of the earth; but if the salt have lost his**
> **savour, wherewith shall it be salted? It is thenceforth good**
> **for nothing, but to be cast out, and to be trodden underfoot**
> **of men. Ye are the light of the world . . . Neither do men**
> **light a candle, and put it under a bushel, but on a candlestick;**
> **and it giveth light unto all that are in the house (Matt 5:13-15).**

Music is a powerful means of communication. Whatever music we listen to, sing, and play broadcasts a message to everyone around us. Your choice, the sacred or the secular, determines that message. Am I stretching things to say that a Christian playing worldly, secular music is like salt without savor, or a candle under a bushel? Therefore, we are given specific commands in the New Testament concerning what kind of music to be involved with:

> **Let the word of Christ dwell in you richly in all wisdom;**
> **teaching and admonishing one another in psalms and hymns**
> **and spiritual songs, singing with grace in your hearts to the**
> **Lord (Col 3:16).**

Psalms, hymns, spiritual songs--this is the kind of music for God's people. It is salt. It is light. It gives a clear, unmistakable witness. There is no mention of secular music here, and for good reason--it just doesn't fit the heart that is filled with the grace of God. If you do **"let the word of Christ dwell in you richly,"** there simply will not be room for worldly, secular music. Another passage puts it this way:

> **And be not drunk with wine, wherein is excess; but be filled**
> **with the Spirit; Speaking to yourselves in psalms and hymns**

> **and spiritual songs, singing and making melody in your**
> **heart to the Lord; Giving thanks always for all things unto**
> **God (Eph 5:18-19).**

Again, psalms, hymns and spiritual songs are the specific types of music commanded, with secular music clearly absent. What other kind of music would one who is **"filled with the Spirit"** possibly produce? With what secular song could we possibly be **"giving thanks always for all things unto God"?**

The whole matter of spiritual gifts enters the picture too. God gives them for the stated purpose: **"to profit withal,"** literally meaning, *"to bring or carry together,"* or, within its context in I Corinthians 12, to draw Christians together to a bond of loving oneness. Would God give spiritual gifts of music to an individual only to have him play and sing secular, worldly music? When have secular songs ever been known to draw Christians together to a bond of loving oneness? In his discussion of the gifts, Paul exhorts, **"Let all things be done unto edifying." (1 Cor 14:26)** Who was ever edified by worldly, secular music that excludes God?

Numerous statements in the Old Testament exhort us to sing and play sacred music. Here are just a few:

> **O come, let us sing unto the Lord: let us make a joyful noise**
> **to the rock of our salvation. Let us come before his presence**
> **with thanksgiving, and make a joyful noise unto him with**
> **psalms (Ps 95:1-2).**

> **Sing unto God, sing praises to his name: extol him that**
> **rideth upon the heavens by his name JAH, and rejoice**
> **before Him (Ps 68:4).**

> **Then will I go unto the altar of God, unto God my exceeding**
> **joy: yea, upon the harp will I praise thee, O God my God (Ps 43:4).**

We have listed only three passages, but were we to list every such exhortation in the Bible concerning music, you would not find even one mention of secular music. And small wonder, for we are commanded:

> **And whatsoever ye do in word or deed, do all in the name of**
> **the Lord Jesus, giving thanks to God and the Father by**
> **him (Col 3:17).**

How can one sing and play worldly, secular music **"in the name of the Lord Jesus"?** And note, we are to do **"all"** in His name.

Further, it is significant that this verse immediately follows the exhortation: **"Let the word of Christ dwell in you richly in all wisdom; teaching and admonishing one another in psalms and hymns and spiritual songs, singing with grace in your hearts to the Lord" (Col 3:16).** There is no getting away from the connection between being filled with the spirit, making sacred music, and doing all things in Jesus' name. Our testimony before the world, and our own relationship with God, hangs, to a significant degree, on the choice we make between the sacred and the secular in music.

36

A CHOICE WORTH CONSIDERING
(PART 3)

In any discussion of the issues of life it is always helpful to back up, take a fresh look at the big picture, and consider the place of each issue in that big picture. Foundational questions are good to ask, questions like: Why did God make us? Why do we exist? What is the meaning of life? Our blessed Lord has not left us without answers to these most important questions:

> **. . . bring my sons from far, and my daughters from the ends of the earth; Even every one that is called by my name: for I have created him for my glory . . . . (Isa 43:6-7).**

Plain enough? We exist for the purpose of glorifying God, therefore, the Apostle Paul gives the all-inclusive exhortation:

> **. . . whatsoever ye do, do all to the glory of God (1 Cor 10:31).**

How does one sing, "I wish they all could be California girls," **"to the glory of God"?** It is rather difficult to think of any secular song that does not give praise, honor, and glory to something other than God. Now think. What does it amount to when someone gives praise, honor, and glory to some "thing" instead of God? Doesn't that sound uncomfortably close to idolatry? Is it possible that God might feel slighted, cheated, betrayed, when His people sing the praises of anything and everything instead of Him? I was discussing these things with an elder brother (a retired missionary) who has a singing ministry, and we both agreed that we feel like we're committing idolatry when we sing a secular song. Therefore, he has made the same choice that I made, to be devoted to sacred music only. My friend, this is no small issue. We serve a jealous God. In the giving of the law to the Israelites the very first commandment is:

> **I am the Lord thy God . . . Thou shalt have no other gods before me . . . for I the Lord thy God am a jealous God . . . . (Ex 20:2-5).**
>
> **For thou shalt worship no other god: for the Lord, whose name is Jealous, is a jealous God (Ex 34:14).**

Recall that the New Testament word **"worship"** literally means, *"to kiss toward,"* and a song of worship is a kiss of affection toward our God. How do you suppose it sits with Him when we, through secular music, offer kisses of affection to other things instead of Him? Israel repeatedly sang the praises of their idols, and provoked God to wrath many times. Isaiah, speaking prophetically, foretells the day when Israel will finally put away their idols:

> **I am the Lord: that is my name: and my glory will I not give to another, neither my praise to graven images. Behold, the former things are come to pass, and new things do I declare: before they spring forth I tell you of them. Sing unto the Lord a new song, and his praise from the end of the Earth . . . let the inhabitants of the rock sing, let them shout from the top of the mountains. Let them give glory unto the Lord, and declare his praise in the islands (Isa 42:8-12).**

How many secular songs can you think of that do not give praise and glory to some *"thing"* instead of God? If it isn't "California Girls," then it's "Puff the Magic Dragon," or "The Yellow Submarine," or "Rudolf the Red Nosed Reindeer." If a song is secular, then, by definition, some *"thing"* always gets the praise and glory instead of God. He is jealous of that praise and glory, and He calls His people to sing **"a new song,"** and it is to be sung **"unto the Lord."** That **"new song"** is to **"give glory unto the Lord,"** and it is to **"declare his praise,"** because He proclaims, **"my glory will I not give to another, neither my praise to graven images."**

In many places the Bible likens our relationship with God to a husband/wife relationship. The church is called the **"bride"** of Christ, and Jesus looks forward to His marriage to His church, His *"called out ones."* We are betrothed to Him. The wedding date is already set, and the wedding feast is being prepared even now. It makes me think of 25 years ago when I was looking forward to my marriage to my bride, the one I chose out of the world to be my own possession. We were betrothed. The wedding date was set and we were busy making all the preparations for the wedding feast. I chose her and set her apart from all other women in the world, and I set my love exclusively on her. I sacrificed my rights, my freedoms, my life as a single person, just so I could share with her all of my time, all my possessions, all of my life. I even gave her my own name, that she might be joined to me for the rest of our lives, to be one. How do you suppose I would have felt if my bride, while in the midst of making preparations for our wedding feast, started singing songs about her old boyfriends? Think about that as you weigh the secular music decision. The great composer, J.S. Bach, went so far as to say:

> *All music should have no other end and aim than the glory of God and the soul's refreshment; where this is not remembered there is no real music but only a devilish hub-bub.*

I think brother Bach must have made the same choice that I'm suggesting, for he headed his compositions: *"J.J." "Jesus Juva"* which means *"Jesus help me."* He ended them *"S.D.G." "Soli Dei gratia,"* which means, *"To God alone the praise."*

37

REMEMBER ESAU

The story of Esau is a sad one which carries many big lessons for us all. One lesson I'd like to focus on is the lesson about values and the exchanges that people make. Esau had something precious, his birthright. Being the firstborn son of Isaac he was in line to be given authority over the family after Isaac's passing. As firstborn Esau would have received a double share of the inheritance. And of greater significance, the very promises of God to the patriarchs were attached to the line of the firstborn. Esau had everything going for him with a great future to look forward to. Then it happened, after a day of unsuccessful hunting, Esau came in from the field feeling faint and hungry. Now Esau surely would not have died of starvation. He had only to wait until supper time. But one whiff of Jacob's red pottage (lentil soup) and Esau just had to have some right now: **"Feed me, I pray thee, with that same red pottage; for I am faint" (Gen 25:30).** But Jacob drove a hard bargain: **"Sell me this day thy birthright" (Gen 25:31).** Imagine, charging such a price for a bowl of soup and a crust of bread. It was very wrong of Jacob to price-gouge his own brother like that. But Esau did not have to agree to it. He could have haggled, or even chosen to wait and look for something to eat elsewhere. But he obviously thought lightly of his birthright, and with little or no hesitation, and a bit of exaggeration, he responded: **"Behold, I am at the point to die: and what profit shall this birthright do to me" (Gen 25:32)?** So he swore to it, had his belly full, rose up, and went his way. And the Bible says: **"Thus Esau despised his birthright" (Gen 25:34).**

In essence, Esau traded the permanent for the temporary. He held a lifetime of blessing and fullness in his hand, and sold it for the momentary relief of a hunger pang. How foolish. How sad. True, the fulfillment of the birthright would have required waiting a span of time, while the red pottage was available immediately. And the option to "buy now/pay later" made the transaction all the more attractive. But when the time came for the birthright and its accompanying blessing to be granted, and Esau fully realized what he lost, oh how he wept. His impulsive, impatient, imprudent decision cost him many bitter tears. More than once the Bible describes those tears. The first time was when Isaac initially told Esau that the blessing was given to Jacob:

> **And when Esau heard the words of his father, he cried with
> a great and exceeding bitter cry . . . . (Gen 27:34).**

And again, when Isaac explained that Jacob would now be lord over Esau, and there was no comparable blessing left to be given to Esau:

> **And Esau said unto his father, Hast thou but one blessing,**
> **my father? bless me, even me also, O my father. And Esau**
> **lifted up his voice, and wept (Gen 27:38).**

The passage goes on to explain that the only thing that Esau could now take comfort in was the thought of killing his brother, Jacob. And the New Testament reveals that Esau was not even able to repent of his foolish decision:

> **For you know how that afterward, when he would have**
> **inherited the blessing, he was rejected: for he found no place**
> **of repentance, though he sought it carefully with tears (Heb**
> **12:17).**

What has all this to do with a musician like you? Everything. Especially for those who excel in it. You will get requests, you will be given offers--you might even be approached by a producer who will promise you stardom and riches. And it will require only a few little compromises. You may have to change the way you dress a bit, your hair style, and perhaps the nature of your music. But if you will play the game his way (so the producer will promise) the money and the fame will be yours, and it won't take long. Just sign the contract.

Oh musician, remember Esau. Truly, the error of Esau has been repeated over and over again by many a singer and musician. They learned to sing in the choir, singing "Amazing Grace." They ministered to souls, they bore testimony to the power of the blood of Christ in the life of a believer. And they became skilled at singing and playing their instrument, so good that a producer took note of their potential, and promised them the world. But once the contract was signed, the compromises began. And before long their Christian witness was all but snuffed out. The hard reality is that true spirituality will never sell like carnality will. Producers generally do not appreciate the reproach of the cross. It tends to narrow the sales market significantly. Spare yourself, O musician, the heartache that so many gifted Christian musicians and singers must bear, who wish they could be a testimony for their Lord who bought them, but their producers will not let them. Under contract they are forced into compromises. Under contract limitations are placed on their music. The words must be softened, the message must be blurred so that the **"narrow way"** that Jesus spoke of does not sound quite so narrow. For we all know that the *real* money does not lie on the **"narrow path,"** it lies on the **"broad path,"** therefore, your music and your appearance must appeal to and appease those on the **"broad path."** Spare yourself the bitter tears that so many musically gifted Christians endure. Don't sell out to the world. Don't trade your rewards in heaven for filthy lucre on earth. Don't barter your birthright for a measly bowl of soup and a crust of bread. Remember your calling. Remember the price that was paid for your redemption. Remember the source of your gifts. Remember the purpose of your gifts. Remember the Lord's promises to the faithful and true. Remember that **". . . profane person, as Esau, who for one morsel of meat sold his birthright (Heb 12:16)."** Interestingly, Esau is called a **"profane person"** here, which is translated from the Greek, *"bebelos,"* meaning *'unhallowed,'* or the opposite of *'sacred,'* or *'. . . that which lacks all relationship or affinity to God' (Vine 490).* You don't want to be in that category. Remember Esau, and remember our Lord's words:

> **No man can serve two masters: for either he will hate the one, and love the other; or else he will hold to one, and despise the other. Ye cannot serve God and mammon (Matt 6:24).**

38

WHO THEN IS WILLING?

The book of 1 Chronicles contains a passage that beautifully typifies the idea of God's people freely choosing to dedicate their possessions and themselves to the Lord. I'm particularly impressed with the way the Bible emphasizes the "willingness" of that choice, and the "joyfulness" of that choice. It was during King David's later life that he found himself troubled over the fact that his house was nicer than God's, so he wanted to build a special **"house of rest for the ark of the covenant" (1 Chron 28:2)**. God was please that David wished to do this. However, because David, as a man of war, had shed much blood, he was not allowed to build God's house of rest. Instead, the job was given to his son, Solomon. David accepted this and gave himself to gathering materials for the house. He informed the whole congregation of Israel of the project that he had in mind, saying: **"Now I have prepared with all my might for the house of my God . . ." (1 Chron 29:2).** David went on to list the materials he had gathered: gold, silver, brass, iron, wood, precious stones, and marble. But he needed more materials, and artificers (skilled craftsmen and artists) to work with the materials, to do the building, to develop a grand, **"exceeding magnifical" (1 Chron 22:5)** dwelling place for the Lord. So David extended the invitation to the people to participate in the project:

> **And who then is willing to consecrate his service this day**
> **unto the Lord (1 Chron 29:5)?**

The response of the people was beautiful:

> **Then the chief of the fathers and princes of the tribes of**
> **Israel, and the captains of thousands and of hundreds, with**
> **the rulers of the king's work, offered willingly (1 Chron 29:6).**

God loves a willing, cheerful giver, and as the people gave abundantly, the Bible says:

> **Then the people rejoiced, for that they offered willingly,**
> **because with perfect heart they offered willingly to the Lord:**
> **and David the king also rejoiced with great joy (1 Chron 29:9).**

David, obviously humbled by this great and *willful* response, was moved to offer a prayer of blessing, thanksgiving, and praise. In that prayer David acknowledges his own insignificance, and his amazement, saying: **"But who am I, and what is my people, that we should be able to offer so willingly after this sort . . ." (1 Chron 29:14).** David is struck by the willingness of the people, and he rehearses his own motivation in the project:

As for me, in the uprightness of mine heart I have willing offered all these things: and now have I seen with joy thy people, which are present here, to offer willingly unto thee (1 Chron 29:17).

Nobody gave because they *had to*. David did not *force* anyone to give. It was with *willing* and *joyful* hearts that God's people consecrated their service to the Lord. They consecrated, dedicated, separated, set apart, their possessions and their skilled labor for the house of the Lord. Their offering that day was followed by a time of worship, and the next day the whole congregation returned to celebrate. Thousands of burnt offerings were sacrificed and a great feast was held, and they **"did eat and drink before the Lord on that day with great gladness . . ." (1 Chron 29:22).**

What lessons this Old Testament event has for us today! This story is a wonderful foreshadowing of the building of God's New Testament house--the church; not the building in which we meet, but the congregation of God's saints, the people. God's church can only be built if His people give of their time, talents, and possessions. He will not force anyone to give, but the same question comes to each of us that David put to the congregation of Israel:

And who then is willing to consecrate his service this day unto the Lord (1 Chron 29:5)?

As a musician, you have a service that can contribute significantly to the building of God's church. But are you willing to separate that service, set it apart, consecrate it, dedicate it, to the building of God's church? And can you do so with a glad heart?

39

The Dedication of a Harp

Several years ago one of my harp customers made a very special request. The family had been attending our harp workshop regularly and the children were learning to play on one of our rental harps, while patiently waiting for the harp they had ordered to be finished. They waited months, as building a harp is a long, slow process. When it was finally done they requested that a formal dedication ceremony be held at the harp workshop. And, since I'm the one who built the harp, they even asked me to lay hands on it and offer a prayer of dedication. We had never done anything like this, but since this family had already made the choice to dedicate themselves to play only music that was pleasing to the Lord, it seemed fitting.

I had no idea of how to go about a harp dedication ceremony. I had never seen such an event before. So I thought it might be helpful to look at how things were dedicated in the Bible. My mind was drawn to the dedication of Solomon's temple. Please understand, I am in no way equating a harp with Solomon's temple. But as I studied the account of this ceremony, there seemed to be some interesting similarities. First, the temple was a big project that took a long time, and so is building a harp, though on a much smaller scale. Second, the completion of the temple was looked forward to with great anticipation, and likewise was the completion of this harp. Next, the Bible explains that after the work on the temple was ended, all the dedicated things were brought in: silver, gold, and vessels. Then the elders and heads of the tribes were assembled, and all the men of Israel, and the congregation of Israel, with the king. Granted, we didn't have a king at our harp workshop, but we did have somewhat of a congregation, with several heads of tribes (families), and the dad of the family receiving this harp was an elder in his church. And the Bible says:

> **And King Solomon, and all the congregation of Israel, that**
> **were assembled unto him, were with him before the ark,**
> **sacrificing sheep and oxen, that could not be told nor**
> **numbered for multitude (1 Kings 8:5).**

It did not seem appropriate for us to make animal sacrifices at this harp dedication ceremony, but a sacrifice of praise on the harp most certainly seemed in order, so we did.

> **And the priests brought in the ark of the covenant of the**
> **Lord unto his place, into the oracle of the house, to the most**
> **holy place, even under the wings of the cherubims (1 Kings 8:6).**

Bear in mind that the **"ark of the covenant"** in the **"most holy place"** was the very dwelling place of God, His presence among His people was right there.

> **And it came to pass, when the priests were come out of the**
> **holy place, that the cloud filled the house of the Lord. So**
> **that the priests could not stand to minister because of the**
> **cloud; for the glory of the Lord had filled the house of the**
> **Lord (1 Kings 8:10-11).**

I have never seen the glory of the Lord in the form of a cloud coming out of a harp and filling a place with the glory of the Lord. I have, however, heard a lot of glorious music coming out of harps and filling a place with the glory of the Lord. And it was at this point that Solomon spoke and explained to the people:

> **. . . The Lord said that he would dwell in the thick darkness.**
> **I have surely built thee an house to dwell in, a settled place**
> **for thee to abide in for ever (1 Kings 8:12-13).**

I surely do not expect the Lord to take up residence (physically) inside a harp, as He did in the temple. But I do know that this harp, and every instrument and voice, is capable of creating a **"house,"** as it were, **"for the Lord to dwell in,"** because the Scripture says:

> **But thou art holy, O thou that inhabitest the praises of**
> **Israel (Ps 22:3).**

God inhabits the praises of His people. He dwells there and takes up residence, as in a house. Every time you sing or play a song of praise you are creating a place for the Lord to inhabit, a house, spiritually speaking, not unlike Solomon's temple. It has been my prayer, ever since I began making harps, that every one of my harps would be used exclusively for this purpose. People today do a lot of things with harps and other instruments, and use them for far lesser purposes, but my vision is that my harps would be tools in the hands of the harper to build **"a house for the Lord to dwell in."** I hope you, as a musician, realize that this gives you a far greater calling than I have. I just make the tools, but you are the skilled workers who use the tools to build a **"house for the Lord to dwell in,"** by playing those praises that He can inhabit.

Perhaps we've stretched things a bit here to make the analogy between Solomon's temple and a harp, but I hope you get the message. That temple was holy, separated, set apart from all that was common, profane, or secular. It was dedicated to be used exclusively for God. May I encourage you, if you haven't done so already, to dedicate your instrument, and yourself, to the same.

PART 7

The Worship Atmosphere

"YE ALSO, AS LIVELY STONES,
ARE BUILT UP A SPIRITUAL HOUSE,
AN HOLY PRIESTHOOD,
TO OFFER UP SPIRITUAL SACRIFICES,
ACCEPTABLE TO GOD BY JESUS CHRIST"
(1 PET 2:5).

40

THE SACREDNESS OF "SACRED" MUSIC

Within the realm of "sacred" music today we have quite an assortment of styles and techniques to pick from. Great controversy surrounds the whole thing, and better men than I have attempted to address the issues. It has been my observation that when music issues are preached about, an emotional reaction often results, creating tension and division between Christians. So I am well aware of the volatile nature of this subject, and have no desire to increase that tension and division. Yet, I feel compelled, at least to try to heighten your awareness, as a musician, of some of the issues at hand.

As mentioned in a previous devotional, many of the questions surrounding "sacred" music are never directly addressed in the Bible. We are, therefore, forced to resort to the use of discernment (judgment) as we endeavor to separate good "sacred" music from bad "sacred" music. Fortunately, the Bible does directly address some issues that can weigh heavily in our discernment of "sacred" music. Recall the very meaning of the word "sacred"—separated, set apart, dedicated, consecrated unto God. In short, "sacred" music is "worship" music, and "worship" music is music that is offered up to God, a holy kiss of affection, a pleasing sacrifice, for His pleasure, His honor, His praise, and the profit and edification of His church. As we attempt to discern the good from the bad, let the "sacredness" or "worshipfulness" of the music be foremost in mind. Too often we are concerned with what pleases me, or my human audience, rather than what pleases God. But "worship" music is, first and foremost, a holy kiss of affection to our Creator, the One that we love with our whole heart, soul, mind and strength. The first question to consider when evaluating "sacred" ("worship") music is: Can God receive this music as a holy kiss of affection?

Stop and consider, O musician, the music that you listen to, sing, and play. Is it indeed "sacred" ("worship") music? Suppose Jesus was to visit your home. Would you feel perfectly comfortable allowing Him to browse through your CD collection? Could you look Him in the eyes while you play and sing along with the same recordings you play in your bedroom or car? How would it feel to play for Him the same songs on your instrument that you play for your friends or audiences?

In reality, these questions are far from hypothetical. The fact is that Jesus does visit your home every day, and every night. He is in your presence all the time.

> **. . . lo, I am with you alway, even unto the end of the world. (Matt 28:2).**

What? know ye not that your body is the temple of the Holy Ghost which is in you, which ye have of God, and ye are not your own? For ye are bought with a price: therefore glorify God in your body, and in your spirit, which are God's (1 Cor. 6:19-20).

The Lord really is in your presence all the time. With your body as His temple He actually does hear all you hear. He hears all you say, all you sing, and all you play. You make the judgment. Does the music in your life have a level of "sacredness," ("worshipfulness") such that it would be fitting to offer up to His Majesty?

41

STRANGE FIRE

It was an awesome sight. Aaron the priest had just put the offerings in place on the altar. There were sin offerings and peace offerings--all sorts of animals killed and dismembered--to be used to make atonement for Aaron himself, and the people. **"And Moses and Aaron went into the tabernacle of the congregation, and came out, and blessed the people . . . ."** (Lev 9:23). Those sacrifices still lay there, unburned. Then it happened. God made His presence and power known to all:

> **. . . and the glory of the Lord appeared unto all the people.**
> **And there came a fire out from before the Lord, and**
> **consumed upon the altar the burnt offering . . . ."** (Lev 9:24).

Can you imagine the terror of such a sight? The Israelites responded the way I think we all would have: **" . . . when all the people saw, they shouted, and fell on their faces"** (Lev 9:24). No human hand had lit that fire, but it was kindled by God Himself. It was divine fire, miraculously produced for the purpose of consuming the offerings of God's people, and it was never to be permitted to die out. God commanded that this sacred fire **"shall not be put out: and the priest shall burn wood on it every morning . . . the fire shall ever be burning upon the altar: it shall never go out. This is the law of the meat offering. The sons of Aaron shall offer it before the Lord, before the altar"** (Lev 6:12-14).

This was the way that God commanded He was to be worshipped--it was **"the law."** And even though He was very specific about many details of the whole thing, Aaron's sons, Nadab and Abihu, tried to approach God another way--their own way. They neglected to use the divine, sacred fire that originated from God. Instead, they used their own, man-made fire:

> **And Nadab and Abihu, the sons of Aaron, took either of**
> **them his censer, and put fire therein, and put incense**
> **thereon, and offered strange fire before the Lord, which he**
> **commanded them not (Lev 10:1).**

Perhaps they figured that fire was fire, and it didn't matter where it came from, but it mattered to God:

> **And there went out fire from the Lord, and devoured them,**
> **and they died before the Lord (Lev 10:2).**

Swiftly, suddenly, and unquestionably, God rejected their sacrifice. And, through Moses, God declared:

> **I will be sanctified in them that come nigh me, and before all the people I will be glorified (Lev 10:3).**

The charred remains of those boys were carried out of the camp, and all Israel bewailed the event. And the Lord spoke to Aaron commanding that he and his sons were not to drink wine or strong drink when they went into the tabernacle, **"And that ye may put difference between holy and unholy, and between unclean and clean" (Lev 10:10).**

There are many lessons we can learn from this event, but the big one is that if God's people are to worship Him in an acceptable way, it must be within certain parameters. One of the great errors of human religions is that people attempt to approach God on their own terms, in their own way, and under their own conditions, which amounts to **"strange fire."** As sincere as many people might be, the God of the Bible does not accept man-made religion. He will be approached on His terms, in His way, and under the conditions that He has specified. If the God of the Bible is to be worshipped acceptably, it must be according to the instructions He has given in His Word. And He has made known to us a number of very specific points to be observed as we worship Him, which we will consider one by one. And bear in mind that one of our main forms of worship is music-- sacred music. And because music is so central to our worship, we would do well to give heed to all that God has to say about worship, lest we find ourselves offering **"strange fire"** to the Lord, having put no **"difference between the unclean and the clean."** I'm not suggesting that God is going to consume with fire anyone who listens to or produces the wrong kind of music. But if we wish to please Him, honor Him, properly represent Him, and properly worship Him, then let us strive to insure that our music fits the atmosphere of worship that He has called for.

42

THE SPIRIT OF A SONG

Music is one of those phenomena that has the marvelous capability of creating an atmosphere, or ambiance, which is sometimes called the "spirit" of a song. The word "spirit" here does not refer to a living being such as an angel or a demon, but to the attitude or mood that is generated within us, and the surrounding environment, as we listen to and produce music. It is that combination of the words, the tune, pitch, tempo, beat, volume, the demeanor of the musician--it all blends together to produce a general, emotional state of mind and heart attitude. The spirit of a song might be that of worship, adoration, sorrow, joy, festivity, anger, wrath, love, hate, compassion, fear, sarcasm, flippancy, sensuality, and such like, or various combinations of these. You can just sense it in the air as the music swells and recedes, and you come away from the music with a certain feeling that you have been impelled to alter your thinking and behavior somehow.

The spirit of a song is an important element for all of us to be very aware of, especially as we attempt to discern the good from the evil in music. The spirit of a song can be good or bad, depending on what the song writer and performer wish to express. When it comes to sacred music, obviously, the spirit of a song ought to be that which honors God and edifies and profits His people. If used appropriately, the spirit of a song can communicate the message of the words with great power.

I will never forget the very first time I heard Handel's <u>Messiah.</u> I was particularly impressed with Handel's ability to match the arrangement of the music with the verses of Scripture he used for the lyrics of the songs. As part one of the oratorio proceeded, song after song talked about Christ's birth and the prophecies that were fulfilled by His birth. It was all so moving, so powerful--the solos, the choruses, the instrumental accompaniment, all masterfully arranged to precisely express the message of each verse. I found the sobriety and the excitement of Messiah's advent to be most captivating as the God honoring and edifying spirit of these songs came through.

Then began part two, a sequence of songs focusing on Christ's suffering and death. An overwhelming sense of sorrow and my own guilt of sin prevailed as these songs spoke of His unjust suffering in my place. As this spirit prevailed I was nearly brought to tears, until, quite abruptly, the mood changed. Right on the heels of the slow, heavy, grave-spirited song, **"And With His Stripes We are Healed,"** came a brief moment of silence. The music then jumped to a light, quick-tempo frivolity as the chorus proclaimed, with an unmistakable spirit of frolic, **"All we like sheep, have gone astray, we have turned every one to his own way."** These phrases repeated over and over in a sing-songy, happy-spirited tune. And I clearly recall thinking to myself, "Handel, what are you doing putting such heavy words to this inappropriate musical arrangement?

Surely you understand the gravity of man's wandering away from God and going his own way. These words are weighty, you have to know better than this." The merry spirit continued as the song rambled on and on, repeating the same phrases again and again, almost too long. But then, just as suddenly as it had changed the first time, the mood changed again. Like slamming on the brakes of a car, the tempo dropped from its lively pace to that of a dirge. The mood flashed from giddy gaiety to mortifying sobriety. Like a ton of bricks, the music came crashing down with those heart-wrenching words, **"And the Lord hath laid on Him the iniquity of us all."** The chorus bewailed it over and over, and before the final words of this verse were sung, those tears that I was previously close to, came forth in a flood. Never had I been so moved by the Gospel message. How brilliantly Handel had arranged this song. It all fell together so wondrously in one moment of time as, to my mind came the picture of a bunch of silly lambs who had wandered away from their shepherd. There they were, dancing and flitting about in a sunny pasture speckled with wildflowers, feeling so energetically liberated to be free of their shepherd's restraints, while totally oblivious to the ravenous lions that lurked in the crevices. What a profound illustration of man's warped view of sin. We think it's fun. We find twisted delight, perverted pleasure in breaking free of God's protective authority. And, like a bunch of silly sheep, we have not the slightest awareness of the devouring intent of the lion-like Tempter, the grief and wrath that sin arouses in our Good Shepherd, and the price that had to be paid for our salvation. Handel's use of "spirit" is what made this song so powerful, so God honoring, so profiting, so edifying. The message of the words was amplified by the arrangement and performance of the music, and there was no inconsistency whatsoever between the lyrics, the arrangement, and the performance. This is the right use of the "spirit" of a song, and it is most appropriate in sacred music.

Sometimes the words of a song might be perfectly fine. Indeed, the words might even be straight from the Bible, but the arrangement of the song and the way it is played and sung still may not necessarily honor God or edify or profit His people. I recall hearing one of my favorite hymns, "O Sacred Head," sung on the radio by one of the most popular, female, Christian recording artists of our day. The hymn itself is generally profound, powerful, and most edifying, but, to my grief, she sang it with a very sensual spirit, making use of sensual techniques such as sliding notes and breathiness. I had also noticed that on her cassette and CD covers this woman is typically dressed immodestly, and maintains a seductive, provocative look on her face. That sensual spirit pervades in her music and reduces the most God-honoring music to the level of night-club sensuality.

In the day and age in which we live, this sensual spirit is something to be very aware of, because its end result is lust. For those who chose to listen to, sing and play sacred music, beware of the sensual spirit that is so common these days. Much sacred music today is defiled by this spirit, and other spirits that neither honor God nor edify or profit His people. Remember, sacred music is worship music, and the end result of worship music ought to be just that--worship.

43

REVERENCE AND GODLY FEAR

It's Sunday morning. Nicely dressed people are scattered about the sanctuary, some sitting, some standing, some shaking hands and chatting, some studying their bulletins. Voices are kept low, subdued--it's Sunday morning. The smiling song leader steps to the platform to greet the congregation while the organist plays the introductory bars to a hymn. A hush comes over the crowd as everybody tries to quickly wrap up his conversation, dropping his voice to a whisper. Late comers slip into the back seats, hoping no one will notice them. The "service" begins with a congregational song. And the atmosphere? Unmistakably, "reverent." And rightly so. Everyone seems to know that you just don't behave the same way at a church "service" as you do at a party. "Reverence" is called for; after all, we are making our formal offering of worship to Almighty God.

There is more to this word, **"reverence,"** than merely keeping our voices down before the service starts. The writer of Hebrews instructs us:

> **. . . let us have grace, whereby we may serve God acceptably**
> **with reverence and godly fear (Heb 12:28).**

So our **"service"** to God, be it a "worship" service, or any other kind of service, if it is to be **"acceptable"** with God, must be with **"reverence and godly fear."** This is part of the atmosphere that God calls for in worship.

Let's look deeper. The word **"reverence"** is translated from the Greek, *"eulabeia,"* which means *"caution" (Vine 532)*. The implication is that we need to be cautious about what we offer up to God in service. This verse (Hebrews 12:28) tells us that there must be caution in what we offer, and how we offer it. And the very next verse tells us exactly why: **"for our God is a consuming fire" (Heb 12:29).** It sort of brings to mind the sons of Aaron, Nadab and Abihu, and their **"strange fire,"** doesn't it? They were literally consumed by the fire of God because they were not reverent (cautious) in their offering to God. And they were not the only ones to receive God's swift and dramatic rejection of their irreverent worship. Cain was not cautious with his offering to God. Recall that things did not go well for Cain. Ananias and Saphira were not cautious in their offering to God, and were smitten on the spot. Both Old Testament and New give strong indication that **"reverence"** (caution) is a must in the worship atmosphere. We must be cautious that our offering to God is something He appreciates, something He called for, and not **"strange fire,"** something we cranked up out of our own carnal hearts.

The God of the New Testament is still **"a consuming fire,"** therefore Heb 12:28 goes on to instruct us that our service to God is not only to be with **"reverence,"** but also with **"godly fear."**

This word **"fear"** is quite an interesting word. It is translated from the Greek, *"deos,"* and I was quite amazed to discover what it actually means—*"fear" (Kubo 234)*. Some Greek manuscripts differ on the original word used here, but they all mean basically the same thing—*"fear."* How interesting! **"Fear"** actually means *"fear."* You know--old-fashioned, knee-knocking, shaking-in-the-boots—**"fear."** Our God is still **"a consuming fire."**

In our present day we tend to think that we are not supposed to actually **"fear"** God any more because we live in the dispensation of grace. But we come across this word **"fear"** in the New Testament, and we have to do something with it, so what we have done is to simply redefine the word. Today, **"fear"** doesn't mean **"fear"** any more, today it means *"awesome respect."* But the trouble is, *"awesome"* doesn't mean *"awesome"* any more. We have redefined that word too. How frequently do we hear statements like, "That's a totally *'awesome'* coat you have on." Or, "We had an *'awesome'* time at the game last night." Today, *"awesome"* can mean anything from slightly above average, to something really great. Granted, the Bible does teach that we have access to the **"throne of grace"** today. We are even told to **"come boldly,"** but not flippantly, or arrogantly, or sarcastically, or sensually. **"Boldness"** must be coupled with **"godly fear,"** and that is not a contradiction, it is balance, it is the only right way to approach God. When we offer our **"service"** to God, our "worship," our kiss of affection, if it is to be **"acceptable,"** it must be with **"reverence and godly fear."** Use caution, O musician, in choosing your music. Be cautious, especially with music that has been written in contemporary times when important words like **"reverence"** and **"fear"** don't mean what they meant when the Bible was written. This is not to say that all contemporary Christian music is bad, because it isn't. Some contemporary works are every bit as good and godly as any music that has ever been written. But we live in a day when the lines have been blurred. Good is called evil and evil is called good. Godliness has been blended with ungodliness. And His Majesty, the Lord Jesus Christ, is often viewed as our "good ol buddy and pal, Jesus." Be discerning, O musician, and separate the good from the evil, the acceptable from the unacceptable. Beware of sacred music that is tainted with arrogance, corrupted with frivolity, or polluted with sensuality. Tune in to the spirit of a song, and offer up nothing to our Holy God but that which is clearly and decidedly characterized by **"reverence and godly fear,"** for this is one part of the worship atmosphere that God calls for.

44

THE BEAUTY OF HOLINESS
PART 1

Have you ever thought of yourself as a **"priest"**? You are one, according to the Bible:

> **Ye also, as lively stones, are built up a spiritual house, an
> holy priesthood, to offer up spiritual sacrifices, acceptable to
> God by Jesus Christ (1 Pet 2:5).**

Note that, as priests, one of our purposes is to offer up **"spiritual sacrifices"** to God. Indeed, the word **"priest"** is defined as *"one who offers sacrifice and has the charge of things pertaining thereto" (Vine 486)*. And certainly, music is among those **"spiritual sacrifices"** that you and I, as priests, offer to God. And note the adjective used to describe the priesthood—**"holy"** *"separation to God" (Vine 306)*. Further note the emphasis on the sacrifices being **"acceptable"** with God. Clearly, in order for a sacrifice to be **"acceptable"** with God, it must be **"holy."** Peter goes on to point out:

> **But ye are a chosen generation, a royal priesthood, an holy
> nation, a peculiar people; that ye should shew forth the
> praises of him who hath called you out of darkness into his
> marvellous light (1 Pet 2:9).**

Note the adjective used to describe the **"nation"** to which we belong—**"holy."** And note another of our purposes: **". . . to shew forth the praises of him . . . ."** Music is certainly one of the ways we can fulfill that purpose, but again, that music must be characterized by holiness. In fact, not only must our music be characterized by holiness, but our whole life must exhibit holiness. Peter explains:

> **As obedient children, not fashioning yourselves according to
> the former lusts in your ignorance: But as he which hath
> called you is holy, so be ye holy in all manner of
> conversation; Because it is written, Be ye holy; for I am
> holy (1 Pet 1:14-16).**

Especially note here that holiness is not relegated to just *some* parts of our lives, such as when we are at church, but **"in all manner of conversation."** And this word **"conversation"** does not just mean talking, it means *"`to conduct oneself,' indicating one's manner of life and character" (Vine 58)*.

Are you getting the picture? Holiness is to be the general character of a Christian, and most certainly prominent during worship. Therefore the psalmist exhorts us:

O worship the Lord in the beauty of holiness: fear before him all the earth (Ps 96:9).

The worship atmosphere, if it is to be acceptable with God, must be holy, which God considers to be a beautiful thing. The word **"holiness"** is translated here from the Hebrew, *"qodesh:"* which means *"separation, place or thing set apart" (Young 487)*. This word is also defined as *"'pure' and 'devoted'" (Vine 113)*. As New Testament priests who offer up sacrifices of praise to God through music, we are obliged to be holy, and to see to it that the music we offer up is holy. Am I stretching things to say that every priest ought to have an air of holiness about him or her? Purity, devotion to godliness, separateness, set apartness, should radiate from our being. Every priest ought to look holy, sound holy, act holy, and be holy.

We who live in this new millennium are blessed to have at our fingertips a wealth of holy music to play. For many centuries holy men and women have authored a vast collection of psalms and hymns and spiritual songs which we can, unhesitatingly, offer up to God in worship as **"spiritual sacrifices,"** and **"shew forth the praises of him"** to one another and to the world. From Old Testament times we have the Song of Moses and the Psalms of David. From earlier New Testament times we have the works of hymn writers such as eleventh century Bernard of Clairvaux. In more recent times we have the works of Isaac Watts, Fanny Crosby, the Wesley brothers, and so many others, right up to the music authors of our present day--godly saints, whose music and lives are characterized by holiness. Such music is perfectly fit to offer up as spiritual sacrifice to shew forth the praises of our holy God.

But, alas, we regrettably find, mingled together with our collection of holy music written by holy authors, some music that is not so holy, written by authors who were, or are, not so holy. Sadly, most hymnals in our churches contain a hymn, for example, that was authored by a song writer who actually persecuted certain groups of Christians. How would you feel about singing that song if your own brother or sister or parent had been jailed and/or executed under that man's regime? Many hymnals contain a hymn that, the music of which, was written by a man who died while shaking an angry fist at God. Our hymnals contain some hymns that misrepresent God, or our relationship with Him. And some hymns are put to an inappropriate tune. The words may be fine, but the tune creates a spirit that does not fit the message of the words. Not to mention a few hymns that were put to the tunes of bar-room songs. Though the "church" has long accepted such works, I would suggest there has been a lack of discernment in some cases. I've not specifically named the hymns or their authors that I see problems with, on purpose, because I want you, the musician, to give this some thought, and arrive at your own conclusions. Prayerfully consider these matters as you seek discernment in what you offer up to God as **"spiritual sacrifices,"** that you may **"worship the Lord in the beauty of holiness."**

45

THE BEAUTY OF HOLINESS
PART 2

O worship the Lord in the beauty of holiness: fear before him all the earth (Ps 96:9).

Have you visited your local Christian bookstore lately? If not, you really should. And while you're there, scan through the tape and CD rack. Take a look at the pictures of the singers and musicians on the covers of the recordings. You'll notice that some of them look very godly, clean, modest, humble. They have sort of a holy glow about them. And you can just about tell by looking at them that their music is godly. The countenance, the expression on the face, the body position, the hair, the clothing, the background scenery--all of it contributes to a general air of holiness about them. The beauty of holiness is manifest in both their appearance and their music, and it is evident that they strive for holiness **"in all manner of conversation."** What a blessing it is to find recordings of this sort on the music rack at the Christian bookstore.

However, you will also find recordings of another sort on that music rack, and probably in greater numbers. Of the male artists, some seem to strive for a certain look, be it the punk look, or whatever is the latest fad. They use the clothing and symbols that the rebellious crowd uses to express their rebellion. You will see bizarre hair styles, skin heads, body piercings, open leather jackets over a T-shirt, and tough-guy stances with the thumbs in the pockets. And the countenance—it just screams *"bad attitude."* The expression on the face is that of rebellion. He looks mean, angry, hostile. He may be hip, he may be cool, he may be tough, in the know, and in style. But is he holy? Is he a picture of purity and devotion to godliness? Is there an air of the beauty of holiness or the fear of God about him? You discern. Does it fit the worship atmosphere that God calls for when we take music from an author like that and offer it up to God as a holy kiss of affection? When God calls for reverence, Godly fear, and the beauty of holiness—does this fit?

We have only considered the male artists, but what of the female? Again, look at the tape and CD covers, but not for too long, because so many are dressed immodestly, when the New Testament specifically commands **". . . that women adorn themselves in modest apparel, with shamefacedness and sobriety; not with broided hair, or gold, or pearls, or costly array; But (which becometh women professing godliness) with good works" (1 Tim 2:9-10).** Some pose with tight, formfitting or revealing clothing, blouses unbuttoned, and the like. And the countenance! So many have an impudent, seductive look on the face. Her hair-do, body positioning, posture, the way she carries herself, everything about her is sexually provocative, with no hint of innocence or purity.

Beyond appearance is the way they sing. Did you ever hear a singer who made you feel like she was trying to seduce you with her voice? Singers can be very sexually provocative. Just by the way they sing they can create a sensual atmosphere. They use certain techniques to do it, such as sliding notes and voice inflections to add sensuality. Or they will put their mouth too close to the microphone and breathe heavily into it while singing to create that breathy effect that is so sexually provocative. Even the way they pronounce certain words, their body gestures--it all contributes to an overall sensual, immoral atmosphere. The words of the songs may be perfectly fine, they may even be Bible verses put to music. But just by they way they sing and present themselves, whatever message the words might contain is drowned out by the message of their life, appearance, and the spirit of their singing.

You discern. Does sensual singing, by a singer who looks rebellious and/or sexually provocative, fit the atmosphere of worship that God calls for, when He requires reverence, godly fear, and the beauty of holiness?

46

DECENCY, ORDER, PEACE

In my high school days I once attended a Led Zeppelin concert with my friends. I was not a Christian at the time, and having grown up on the rock music of the 60's, this was one of my favorite groups. I enjoyed their music on the radio, and had a couple of their recordings at home. Yet, I did not find their concert to be enjoyable. It was held at Boston Gardens, and the place was packed. They used enormous speakers that were cranked up full blast. It was painfully loud. The beat thundered with bone-rattling intensity while the lead singer frequently made an assortment of ear-piercing screams and screeches into the microphone. It hurt, and there was no way to turn the volume down. The songs were largely unrecognizable, just a chaotic bombardment of very uncomfortable noise and high-stress distortion and confusion that inundated the crowd. I wanted to get out, but for the sake of my friends I endured the whole thing, and went home rather numb, in need of an aspirin. Maybe that experience contributed to my present appreciation for harp music.

I shared all that just to set up a contrast between music that fits, and music that does not fit the worship atmosphere that God calls for:

> **For God is not the author of confusion, but of peace, as in all churches of the saints (1 Cor 14:33).**

This verse is taken from a passage in which the Apostle Paul is specifically describing the order of a worship service for the New Testament church. If ever we have clear instructions about how to worship God acceptably, it is in this passage. Note the key elements here, the absence of **"confusion"** and the presence of **"peace."** Paul continues his instructions pointing out that each member is to share his gift in an orderly way that builds faith and produces peace, without confusion. And he concludes with:

> **Let all things be done decently and in order (1 Cor 14:40).**

Since music is one of our main forms of worship, it seems right to apply all this to music. If God wants a worship service to be devoid of confusion, characterized by peace, conducted decently and in order, don't you think our music ought to be that way too?

Within the sphere of contemporary Christian music large numbers of artists have patterned themselves after the popular secular music artists of our heathen society. We have Christian Rock, Christian Punk, Christian Rap, Christian Heavy Metal, Christian Thrash Metal, etc. I do not wish to make any judgments of these artists concerning their motives. I'm sure that at least some of them are sincerely trying to reach a crowd that would never attend a regular church service or hymn sing. But consider the message that predominates when, for example, a Christian rock band dresses with the same attire as a secular rock group, or even a Satanic rock group. The musicians adorn themselves with the same symbolic adornments as the worldly and Satanic groups. They play their instruments in the same way with the same excessively loud wailing beat and the same frequent use of distortion. And sometimes they carry out the same sensual, sexually suggestive antics that a secular rock group does. Some even demonstrate the anger and violence of throwing and/or smashing their guitars on stage. Some of the names of the Christian groups and song titles are just as gruesome and disgusting as those of the secular groups. And the things that go on at some Christian rock concerts are the same as at a secular rock concert. There is stage diving where people literally dive from the stage into the crowd. There is body surfing where people are held up overhead and passed around by the crowd. There is moshing (also called slam dancing) where people make a dance of violently slamming their bodies into one another. In his book, *Measuring the Music*, John Makujina quotes moshing participants making statements such as:

> *It looks like one huge brawl…violent fun…any aggressions you have, you let them out…I don't feel fulfilled if I don't come away with a scratch or a bloody nose…Nothing you could do [while slam dancing] could be socially unacceptable. You could walk up and pound someone in the face, and it's all in good fun (Makujina 49).*

The lead vocalist for a Christian rock group is quoted as saying:

> *If the churches book us, they usually know what to expect. We're not timid about what we do. It's a rock concert.*

Another band member continues:

> *Yes, it looks like a rock concert, it sounds like a rock concert, and in every aspect except for the lyrics, it's just like any standard rock concert by today's teen-oriented bands: plenty of flash and lots of thrash on stage; heads bobbing and bodies moshing in the crowd (Makujina 52).*

One band was even quoted as giving this *"exhortation"* to the crowd:

> *If you're happy and you know it, bang your head (Makujina 53).*

Consider the pervading message of a presentation like that. Even if you could understand the words to the songs, whatever message those words might contain is seriously overshadowed by the conflicting message of everything else in the production which screams rebellion and general ungodliness. And consider how utterly contrary all of this is to the Biblical exhortation to have decency, order and peace at a time of worship. And remember that **". . . God is not the author of confusion, but of peace, as in all churches of the saints" (1 Cor 14:33).** If God is not the author of all the confusion and mayhem of this music, who do you suppose is? And if God commands us to **"Let all things be done decently and in order" (1 Cor 14:40),** how do you suppose it sits with Him when his people participate in events like this in the name of *"worship?"* You discern whether this sort of thing fits the worship atmosphere that God calls for, when He requires reverence, godly fear, the beauty of holiness, decency, order, and peace.

47

IN SPIRIT AND IN TRUTH
(PART 1)

She was sure her people had the corner on worship. If worship was to be acceptable it had to be done at the mountain of Samaria, where her fathers had worshipped. The Jews, who thought that worship ought to take place in Jerusalem, had it all wrong, in her mind. Jesus perceived that this woman at Jacob's well needed some help in understanding acceptable worship, so He told her:

> **Woman, believe me, the hour cometh, when ye shall neither**
> **in this mountain, nor yet at Jerusalem, worship the Father.**
> **Ye worship ye know not what: we know what we worship;**
> **for salvation is of the Jews. But the hour cometh, and now is,**
> **when the true worshippers shall worship the Father in spirit**
> **and in truth: for the Father seeketh such to worship him (Jn 4:23).**

Geographical location has nothing to do with making worship acceptable, according to Jesus. God is seeking worshippers, but the ones He is after are those who do so in **"spirit and truth."** He explains:

> **God is a Spirit; and they that worship him must worship**
> **Him in spirit and in truth (Jn 4:24).**

God is not bound by the limitations of the physical realm, for He is Spirit. To make contact with Him does not require a trek to some physical location for the carrying out of a set of rituals. God will not necessarily be found by getting in your car and driving to a certain mountain, shrine, or church building. God is Spirit, and contact with Him happens in the spiritual realm, regardless of geographical location. Prayer, meditation, Bible study, and song are the vehicles that bring us in contact with God. This is where worship happens. When His Spirit reaches down to ours, and our spirit reaches up to His, we touch, we commune, we fellowship, we agree, we blend, we know, we love, we adore—we worship, **"in spirit and in truth,"** heart to heart, Spirit to spirit, as Jesus said it would be:

> **At that day ye shall know that I am in my Father, and ye in**
> **me, and I in you (Jn 14:20).**

Are you getting the sense of the spiritual dimension of the worship atmosphere? The Apostle Paul speaks of this spiritual contact:

> **. . . ye have received the Spirit of adoption, whereby we cry,**
> **Abba, Father. The spirit itself beareth witness with our**
> **Spirit, that we are the children of God (Rom 8:15-16).**

Again, note the emphasis on spiritual contact, His Spirit **"beareth witness"** with our spirit. If worship is to be acceptable, this spiritual contact must happen, and song is a wonderful way to draw our spirit to His. Of course, song is no guarantee of worship, because it can easily happen that someone may play and/or sing a song and remain unconscious of the meaning of the words. I marvel at how many people who do not believe in God can sing Christmas carols that are loaded with theological truths, yet, they are not aware that they are singing words they don't believe. And as Christians, we too can play and sing spiritual songs, mouthing profound words, while our thoughts are focused on the lunch menu, or the new car, the shopping list, the handsome guy who just sat down in the pew in front of us, or whatever. But if we sing and play in a conscious way, and the words become the expression of our hearts, then worship is happening and our spirit is in contact with God's. Thus we are exhorted:

> **. . . be filled with the Spirit; speaking to yourselves in psalms**
> **and hymns and spiritual songs, singing and making melody**
> **in your heart to the Lord (Eph 5:19).**

It is the filling of the spirit that gives rise to the song and melody of the heart, which produces the worship of God **"in spirit."** And bear in mind that **"melody"** in the original language refers to playing a stringed instrument, making all of this totally applicable to the musician. Therefore, strive, O musician, to worship, to play, to sing, with your thoughts focused on the words of the songs you do. Strive to make those words, and the tune they are put to, the expression of your heart, for **"the true worshippers shall worship the Father in spirit and in truth: for the Father seeketh such to worship him" (Jn 4:23).**

48

IN SPIRIT AND IN TRUTH
PART 2

In His conversation with the woman at the well Jesus not only told her that those who worship God must worship Him **"in spirit,"** but He also mentioned that true worship must be **"in truth."** Obviously, the words that are expressing the attitude of our hearts must be **"true"** words. They must express true doctrine. The words to our songs must give a true representation of God, of us, and of our relationship with God. Unfortunately, it cannot be assumed that every song the church accepts is a song of truth. There are songs accepted by churches that contain heresy, false statements, and untruth. There are songs accepted by churches, songs included in hymnals, songs written by Christians, that misrepresent God, or us, or our relationship with Him. Of the chief offenders, there are, what I call, the happy-sappy, lovey-dovey, mushy-gushy romance songs. In an effort to emphasize the love-relationship that Christians have with God, some song writers have composed songs that portray God and the Christian as two starry-eyed lovers, strolling dreamily through a rose garden, hand in hand, whispering sweet nothings into one another's ears. It is true that **"love"** is central to our relationship with God. And Scripture uses the marriage relationship to illustrate certain aspects of that love relationship, such as submission, loyalty, faithfulness, loving care, protection, provision, etc. But the mushy-gushy Hollywood romance of human marriage is never found in the Bible between God and a human being. Christ had no such relationship with any of His followers. We would do well to consider refraining from any songs that portray our relationship with God as a Hollywood romance, because it is not **"in truth."** In describing the various aspects of the usage of the word **"love"** throughout the Bible, the Wycliff Bible Encyclopedia divides **"love"** into three categories, the love of God to man, man to God, and man to man. In the section on the love of man to man, it is emphasized:

> *This love, which must be distinguished from erotic and romantic affection, is the logical counterpart of the divine love toward man (Wycliff 1054).*

Well said. The love between the Christians is patterned after the love between God and the Christian, and both are to the exclusion of any sense of *erotic* and *romantic* love. Any song, therefore, that is tainted by a sense of Hollywood romance is untruth because it does not accurately represent our relationship with God.

Another aspect of our relationship with God that is sometimes misrepresented in songs is *"friendship."* Some songs depict God as our *"good-ol buddy and pal."* This occurs particularly songs written in modern times when God's Sovereign Highness, His Lordship, His Authoritative Majesty, tend to be de-emphasized. It is true that friendship is spoken of in the Bible as part of our relationship with God, but not at the expense of His Lordship and the clear distinction between His Highness and our lowness. Throughout Scripture, when godly men worshipped we commonly find them bowing down, kneeling, prostrated, giving clear recognition of God's Highness and their lowness. David exhorts:

> **O come, let us worship and bow down: let us kneel before the Lord our maker. For he is our God; and we are the people of his pasture, and the sheep of his hand . . . . (Ps 95:6-7).**

We find no sense of bringing God down to our level, no familiarity, no *"good-ol buddy"* mentality. Even in cases when a man stood to pray, rather than kneeling, such as when Solomon dedicated the temple, his words, and the spirit of his words, still gave definite acknowledgement to God's Sovereign Majesty. So, you discern, O musician. Do songs fit that portray our relationship with God as a happy-sappy, lovey-dovey, mushy-gushy, Hollywood romance? Are songs fitting that present God as our good-ol buddy and pal? Is this **"in truth?"** Does such misrepresentation fit the worship atmosphere that God calls for, when He requires that worship be in spirit and in truth, with reverence, godly fear, the beauty of holiness, decency, order, and peace?

Fortunately, we have an abundance of songs that portray the love and friend relationship between us and God in an appropriate way, at no expense to His Sovereign Highness. We do not have to sacrifice truth in order to emphasize God's love and friendship. Give yourself, O musician, to music that accurately represents God, us, and our relationship with Him, for **". . . the true worshippers shall worship the Father in spirit and in truth: for the Father seeketh such to worship him" (Jn 4:23).**

49

OUR ONENESS WITH CHRIST

The question may be raised, "Why can't I just enjoy the music I like, and simply *not* offer it up to God as worship?" It's a valid question, for who ever said that *every* song we ever listen to, or play or sing, necessarily has to be offered up to God as worship?

But let's consider a few fundamental principles as we look at this question. To begin, the Bible makes it clear that, as Christians, we are **"one"** with Christ:

> **. . . he that is joined unto the Lord is one spirit (1 Cor 6:17).**

In this passage, this fundamental principle is the stated reason for why a Christian cannot simply *enjoy* immorality, and leave God out of the picture for a while:

> **Know ye not that your bodies are the members of Christ?**
> **Shall I then take the members of Christ, and make them the**
> **members of an harlot? God forbid (1 Cor 6:15).**

Because we are one with Christ, and our bodies are members of Christ, whatever we do, we cause Christ to do with us. We cannot simply disconnect our selves from Him, go and enjoy sin, and then come back to fellowship whenever we choose. This is a big principle, and it applies to everything we do in life. Paul is addressing the specific issue of immorality in this passage, but that is just one application of the principle of oneness. In the big picture, this principle applies across the board. Paul continues:

> **What? know ye not that he which is joined to an harlot is**
> **one body? For two, saith he, shall be one flesh. But he that is**
> **joined unto the Lord is one spirit (1 Cor 16:16-17).**

The principle is that if a person is a Christian, he is therefore joined to the Lord, and therefore he is one spirit with Christ. Shall we then become one with a harlot, making Christ one with the harlot also? God forbid! Likewise, shall we then expose ourselves to ungodly music that violates the principles of worship that God calls for, and subject Christ to that ungodly music too? We force Him to listen to whatever music we listen to, or sing or play. He is *with* us at all times. He is *in* us at all times. There is no getting away from Him:

> **What? know ye not that your body is the temple of the Holy**
> **Ghost which is in you, which ye have of God, and ye are not**
> **your own (1 Cor 16:19)?**

Your body is His house. He lives there. He goes where you go. If you attend a rock concert, so does He. You cannot leave Him home while you go out. You cannot tell Him to go away on vacation while you go enjoy an evening of ungodly music. Paul concludes this passage with another all-inclusive principle:

For ye are bought with a price: therefore glorify God in your body, and in your spirit, which are God's (1 Cor 16:20).

There is no part of life that this principle does not apply to. Because we are one with Him, and we are bought, at the price of His blood, and we are not our own. We owe it to Him to glorify Him, not shame Him. We owe it to Him to please Him, not grieve Him. We owe it to Him to bless Him, not annoy Him. O musician! There is such a wealth of good, sacred music that Christ is blessed with, honored with, glorified with. You don't need the other, and neither does He. Remember His presence every time you make or listen to music.

50

THE SUBJECT MATTER OF SONGS

Within the parameters of sacred music we have songs written about a wide variety of subjects. In these modern times the spectrum of subject matter seems to be ever-widening, and sometimes the appropriateness of certain subjects may be rather questionable, so discernment is needful. Again, if we keep in mind the worship atmosphere that God calls for, it should not be so difficult to settle on which subjects fit that atmosphere, and which do not. We have only to ask: Does the subject matter of this song fit God's requirements for reverence, Godly fear, the beauty of holiness, decency, order, peace, in spirit and in truth? Is the subject matter of this song something our Lord will appreciate listening to, and be blessed by? Will the subject matter of this song **"edify"** God's church and **"profit withal,"** drawing us together to a loving bond of oneness?

The Bible itself records numerous songs that we can look to for examples of appropriate subject matter. All of the Psalms are songs. The Book of Revelation contains songs that are actually sung in heaven around God's throne. As we consider the appropriateness of subject matter for songs, it seems wisdom that we study the songs that God Himself listens to in heaven, because we know for certain that He approves of them. The Song of Moses, for example, is sung in heaven by the tribulation overcomers. In great numbers they stand on the sea of glass mingled with fire, and to the accompaniment of the harps of God, they sing:

> **. . . Great and marvelous are thy works, Lord God almighty;**
> **just and true are thy ways, thou King of saints. Who shall**
> **not fear thee, O Lord, and glorify thy name? for thou only**
> **art holy: for all nations shall come and worship before thee;**
> **for thy judgments are made manifest (Rev 15:3-4).**

Consider the nature of these words. They talk about the great things that God has done, His holiness, His righteous judgment, His holy character. We can't miss if we do songs with lyrics like that.

Another song of heaven is sung by the four beasts (living ones), along with the four and twenty elders, who fall down before the Lamb. To the accompaniment of harps they sing this new song:

> **Thou art worthy to take the book, and to open the seals**
> **thereof: for thou wast slain, and hast redeemed us to God by**
> **thy blood out of every kindred, and tongue, and people, and**
> **nation; And hast made us unto our God kings and priests:**
> **and we shall reign on the earth (Rev 5:9-10).**

This song talks about His excellence, His worthiness, and our redemption in Christ. Notice, **". . . for thou wast slain, and hast redeemed us to God by thy blood . . . ."** One of the themes they sing about in heaven is the blood atonement, and I suspect that this subject will be a prominent song theme throughout eternity. Unfortunately, in our present day, some Christian groups have drifted away from songs about the blood atonement. Some even consider it too gruesome to sing about. It has been my observation that as a church (or an individual) grows lukewarm or cold toward God and the things of God, one of the first things to go is the songs about the blood. As apostasy creeps in, songs about the blood drift out. But if the blood atonement is a central song theme in heaven, so it ought to be for us on earth. Think about the centrality of the blood atonement for the Christian, for Christ's blood is the very core of the Christian faith:

- It was Christ's blood that paid the legal penalty for our crimes against God.

- It was Christ's blood that spared us God's wrath.

- It was Christ's blood that satisfied God's justice.

- It was Christ's blood that bought us out of the slave market of sin.

- It was Christ's blood that gave us power to overcome Satan, the accuser of our brethren.

Leave out the blood atonement, and you leave out all hope of salvation, and any chance of a right relationship with God. Consider what we have in Christ:

> **. . . we have redemption through his blood, the forgiveness of sins, according to the riches of his grace (Eph 1:7).**

> **Wherefore remember, that ye being in time past Gentiles . . . without Christ, being aliens from the commonwealth of Israel, and strangers from the covenants of promise, having no hope, and without God in the world: But now in Christ Jesus ye who sometimes were far off are made nigh by the blood of Christ (Eph 2:11-13).**

This is why we need songs about the blood atonement. We must **"remember"** who we are, where we came from, and what brought us into a right relationship with God. O musician, drift away from anything else, but don't drift away from songs about the blood atonement of Christ. When you listen to music, when you play your instrument, when you sing, when you compose your own songs, **"remember"** the blood atonement, as do the beasts and the elders, and the ten thousand times ten thousands of angels of heaven who sing:

Worthy is the Lamb that was slain to receive power, and riches, and wisdom, and strength, and honour, and glory, and blessing. And every creature which is in heaven, and on the earth, and under the earth, and such as are in the sea, and all that are in them, heard I saying, Blessing, and honour, and glory, and power, be unto him that sitteth upon the throne, and unto the Lamb for ever and ever. And the four beasts said, Amen . . . . (Rev 5:12-14).

BIBLIOGRAPHY

Emurian, Ernest K., *Living Stories of Famous Hymns*. Grand Rapids: Baker, 1955.

Encarta Encyclopedia. CD Rom: Microsoft Corp. 1993-2001.

Funk & Wagnalls New Practical Standard Dictionary. 2 vols. NY: Funk & Wagnalls, 1952. Now publ. at J.G. Ferguson and Assoc., Chicago.

Kubo, Sakae, A *Reader's Greek-English Lexicon of the New Testament*, Grand Rapids: Andrews Univ. Press and Zondervan Publ. House, 1975.

Makujina, John, *Measuring the Music*, Willow Street, Pa.: Old Paths Publ., 2002.

Osbeck, Kenneth, *101 More Hymn Stories*, Grand Rapids: Kregel Publ., 1985.

Vine, Unger, White, *Vine's Complete Expository Dictionary of Old and New Testament Words*, Nashville: Thomas Nelson, Inc. Publ., 1985.

Wycliffe Bible Encyclopedia, Chicago: Moody Press, 1975.